VET

Hugh Lasgarn
mining village
nary College. Since graduating, he
and worked in the Welsh Border country that
he loves and where he met and married his
wife. His first book, *Vet in Green Pastures*, was
an instant success on its publication in 1985,
and the subsequent volumes, *Vet for All Seasons*
and *Vet in a Storm*, have established him as a
hugely popular writer with a rather different
story to tell.

HUGH LASGARN

Vet in a Village

FONTANA/Collins

To Simon, Oliver and
Emma Louise

First published by Souvenir Press Ltd 1988
First issued in Fontana Paperbacks 1989

Copyright © 1988 by Hugh Lasgarn

Printed and bound in Great Britain by
William Collins Sons & Co. Ltd, Glasgow

All creatures have a right to survive in God's world in a way as conducive to their well-being, both mental and physical, as possible.

HUGH LASGARN
November 1987

1

The house was called Gatewood. Situated halfway between the church and the Red Lion, it was convenient for both kinds of spirit!

It was set back from the lane between two half-timbered cottages, of which there were many in the village, often dating back to the fourteenth century; the picturesque setting of Welbury was a marked contrast to the forbidding environment of the Abergranog of my youth.

The reason for our move from Ledingford to a village nearer the Welsh Border was twofold: firstly, it was advantageous to the practice to be more available to the clients in that area, the furthest being twenty miles from the main surgery; secondly, although I was now a partner, I still wanted to retain a degree of independence, and developing a personal niche in the countryside was one way of achieving it.

Maybe there was a third reason which I was reluctant to admit, and that was that I was now closer to the hills of 'lumpy' Wales, for which I still retained an abiding affection.

Diana and the girls were excited with the move; for them, it was the prelude to an immensely happy time with the girls growing up in a solid rural community where honest values still seemed in vogue and the natural beauty of the surroundings was as yet unspoilt.

Of course, the degree of isolation meant I was permanently on call, reminding us that being a vet – and a vet's wife – was a way of life and not a job.

It started on the very day we moved in. The furniture van was disgorging our goods and chattels when the phone rang.

'The police!' said Diana nervously. 'What have you done?'

I took the receiver.

'Ledingford Station, Mr Lasgarn. We've had a message that a bull has been in collision with a car at Barnfield Oak. The sergeant on the spot says it should be put down. Will you attend?'

'Barnfield Oak?' I queried.

'Four miles out of Welbury on the Brecon Road, right at the junction.'

'I know it,' I said. 'Yes, I'll go over now!'

Diana stood despondent amid the chaos.

'Not a call?' she said, disbelievingly.

'A bull on the loose has been knocked down, I've got to go and shoot it!'

'What a start, Hugh!' she said wearily.

It did seem a bit much that my first consultation as a village vet should involve shooting the patient, but one could never expect emergencies to order; so somewhat guiltily leaving Di to cope amid cat, kids and candlesticks, I set forth for Barnfield Oak.

After about ten minutes, I encountered a sharp bend where my eye caught a 'POLICE. ACCIDENT' sign on the verge. Rounding the corner I came upon a queue of cars and lorries, but slipped cautiously by until I arrived at the scene and pulled to the side.

The car involved, a small Standard Eight saloon, stood just in front of me with its roof and bonnet dented, windscreen smashed and bumper twisted like a corkscrew. The driver, a local publican suffering from 'shock', had vanished, and the circumstances became a little clearer when I overheard a small fellow in a tweed hat and oil-stained overalls say he wouldn't want to put a naked flame near the car – and it wasn't because of leaking petrol!

He was leaning on a dilapidated pick-up wagon with 'Totty's Garage' written on the side, and was in fact Totty himself. I had to admit that even though we were 'in the sticks' the services seemed pretty efficient, and when I saw a vicar appear, wheeling a bicycle, I really was impressed.

A policeman, also standing by a bicycle, was taking notes, so I got out and, grabbing my case, went over to him.

'Vet!' I announced.

He looked up.

'Mr Lasgarn,' he said, smiling cheerfully. "'Ow nice to see you!' and proffered a massive hand.

'PC Packham!' I said with surprise. 'What are you doing out here?'

'Out to grass,' he said. 'Now that you've come to Welbury, I'm yer local bobby.'

That was great news, for Bob Packham and I had been involved in many incidents when he was stationed in Ledingford. We got on well together and the fact that I was on his patch was going to be a big help.

'What's to know?' I asked.

'Only just come meself,' he replied. 'Z-Car 'Arry was here first!'

He nodded his head back towards a shining white Ford Zodiac, its radio crackling away importantly. 'Traffic Department. Can't touch 'em since they got a new set of wheels. Me! I got a job to get a new washer for me pump!'

It was obvious by Bob's tone that a degree of enmity existed between the two factions and was confirmed by the attitude of the sergeant who now joined us.

'Want this job cleared up quickly,' he said, without any formal introduction. 'Traffic's been held up long enough. Got any information who owns it, Packham?'

'I do!' came a voice, and a roughshaven character, sporting half-specs, flat cap and a mac tied with string, hobbled up.

'Thought he was yourn, Artie,' said Bob Packham. "'Ow did he get loose?'

'Donkey let 'im out!' said the old man.

'You ain't got no donkey,' chipped in Totty.

'Bloody donkey who left me gate open – sorry, Vicar,' he replied grumpily. 'That's who let him out.'

I moved on past the crumpled Standard Eight to where

the bull was lying. He was a big fellow: a Hereford and all of fifteen hundredweight.

'Brain damage,' said the sergeant. 'Finish him off and we'll tow him to the side.'

'I want to examine him first,' I retorted firmly and, kneeling down, commenced to do so.

Apart from a trickle of blood at his nose, there were few signs of injury, just some minor abrasions on the shoulder and a piece missing from the tip of his right horn. There were no broken bones or damaged ribs and he just lay there, breathing softly and staring unblinkingly into space.

'Clear the people back, Packham!' snapped the sergeant. 'Let's get on with it!'

'I want to test the reflexes,' I announced.

'What?' The sergeant snorted impatiently.

'It just might be concussion,' I explained and, opening my case, took out a large hypodermic needle.

'Best bloody bull I ever 'ad – sorry, Vicar,' said Artie.

'Hard to bear,' said the vicar solemnly. 'Hard to bear.'

'Ought to put more time in church, Vicar, didn' he?' chipped in Totty.

'I was at 'Arvest Festival,' said Artie, grumpily. 'Didn' do much bloody good – sorry, Vicar. Did it?'

It was at that point that I stuck the needle into the bull's skin just on mid-spine.

The effect was astounding.

It was as if I had connected him to the high voltage mains, for he juddered like a demented dynamo, bounded to his feet and charged headlong into the shining white Zodiac. The sound was horrific as the vehicle's wheels left the ground and in seconds its front had been remodelled into quite a bizarre design, the shattered lights hanging like gouged eyes from their sockets.

Not content with one assault, though it was more than adequate, he smashed it hard again, then stood back a pace to admire his handiwork before whisking his tail and trotting off up the road.

Save for the tinkling slivers of headlamp glass falling to

10

the ground and the gentle hiss as one of the tyres deflated, there was silence. Nobody moved or uttered a word.

Then the vicar said, 'The Lord be praised!' which I assumed was for the bull's recovery and not for the damage to the Zodiac.

Artie started to chuckle.

'I'd better get after 'im,' he said. 'Don' want the bugger – sorry, Vicar – to do any more damage.' He hobbled off. 'I'll remember you for this, Mr Lasgarn,' he shouted.

'So will I, Mr Lasgarn!' It was the voice of the Traffic Sergeant, 'Z-Car Harry', who was standing menacingly behind me. 'So will I!'

'I'll get the particulars, shall I, Sergeant?' said PC Packham, hardly able to contain himself.

'Anything I can do?' asked Totty, grinning all over his face. 'Give you a good price for both the wrecks!'

The sergeant glowered fiercely at him and then turned on me.

'I'll follow them up,' I suggested, before he could say anything. 'Just in case they need me.' And, picking up my case and threading my way carefully through the broken glass, I thankfully set off after Artie and his bull.

* * *

That incident firmly established my presence in the area in a manner that far exceeded direct advertising, even if it had been permitted. Indeed, it was no wonder everyone knew about it, in view of the fact that the main participants were a publican, a well-known farming character, a chatty garage owner, the local bobby and the vicar. The latter even welcomed us to the village from the pulpit, during Sunday Service – though I was not there to hear it!

I bought my petrol at Totty's Garage and, just by chance, notched up another prestige point on his forecourt quite soon after the bull episode, when he asked me to examine his dog.

It was a rather moth-eaten German Shepherd called Tramp, which was quite apt considering its appearance.

'What d'ye reckon this is?' enquired Totty, lifting up one of Tramp's forelegs and exposing the elbow. 'Had it some time. Same on the other leg, too.'

He was referring to a large callous over the joint, completely devoid of hair and well established.

'Bad ears,' I said.

Totty tilted his head to one side like an inquisitive pheasant and blinked in similar fashion.

'Bad ears!' he repeated. 'This?' He held the elbow up higher, nearly toppling Tramp over in the process.

'I'll show you,' I said and, raising Tramp's ear flap, revealed an inflamed, wax-filled orifice. 'They are very irritating and the only relief he can get is by scratching,' I explained slowly. 'When he does that, he rests one elbow on the concrete while he scratches the opposite ear with his other foot – that causes the abrasion.'

Totty let Tramp go and stood up.

'That's very clever, Mr Lasgarn,' he said, admiringly. 'Very clever indeed.'

I cleaned out Tramp's ears and gave Totty some ointment for further treatment before driving off and leaving a very favourable impression as to my diagnostic ability.

I failed to mention, of course, that my apparently psychic powers were due to Tramp performing his antics right in front of my car on the very first day I called for petrol.

* * *

Though my success with the concussed bull had contributed to my reputation, it was a very different accident victim that brought me back to earth, within my first week.

It came about through a small boy who knocked at my door with an owl in a shoe box.

'Found him in the grass at the back of the church,' he said. 'Jus' sat there an' let me pick him up, but he don' look very well.'

Carefully I lifted the feathery bundle from the container. It was a Little Owl and a youngish one at that. Its wings extended readily, legs appeared sound and I could detect

12

no apparent sign of injury. If it was concussed, certainly its eyes gave no clue, for they were wide and static.

'Will he live?' asked the lad anxiously.

'Any wild bird that lets itself be picked up and put in a shoe box must be pretty sick,' I told him. 'I think this little chap looks to have concussion. He must have collided with something.'

'I thought they could see in the dark,' said the lad.

'Better in the dark than the light, though they fly from memory mostly,' I explained. 'But he's young and inexperienced and might have got his timing wrong. What's your name?'

He told me it was Percy and that he was from the council estate.

'Well, Percy,' I said. 'Let's see if we can revive him with some glucose solution.'

I mixed a teaspoonful in some warm water and with the lad's help fed the Little Owl with the aid of a dropper. Then I filled a hot water bottle, covered it with a blanket and placed the patient in its shoe box, on top.

'Best keep him here tonight,' I told Percy. 'Come back tomorrow and he should be much better.'

'I want to keep him if I can,' he said brightly. 'Train him to come to me an' that.'

Certainly the little creature would need some extra care over the next few weeks until it was stronger and I could see no wrong in the suggestion. So Percy went away, promising to return the following evening.

Next day the owl was much perkier, but still made no effort to stretch its wings.

During the day I made several attempts to stimulate it by gently tossing it in the palms of my hands, but not the slightest flutter did it make. About four o'clock, when I returned from my calls, I decided to take it into the garden to allow the air to freshen its feathers.

It sat contentedly in the palms of my hands, glaring up with its brilliant yellow eyes, but offered no response.

Then suddenly, Branston, my Jack Russell, came bounding and barking across the lawn to see what I was up to.

Hearing the commotion, the owl took off immediately and flew to the top of a telegraph pole just across the lane – the effect of Branston being like my needle on the bull's back.

The trouble was that whilst I was pleased with the tiny creature's recovery, I suddenly remembered Percy's intentions to keep it.

There was going to be a very disappointed little boy, later that evening.

He stood there looking up at the pole, his back was towards me so that I was unable to see his face.

'Isn't that good?' I said. 'He must be better to fly up there.'

Percy did not say anything, he just kept his eyes fixed on the tiny creature, who at one point looked down to him in an uncannily familiar way.

'I expect he will go back to his roost when it's dark,' I went on, putting my hand on Percy's shoulder. 'Then once he gets his confidence again, he will probably go off hunting for his supper.' But I knew I was just talking for the sake of it and as I rambled on I felt his little body begin to shake.

Then he turned and looked up at me, his eyes full, the tears poised to run down his pale cheeks.

'He was my h'owl, an' you let 'im go!' he sobbed. 'If he was better you didn' 'ave to let him go!'

'But he's a wild creature, Percy. He wouldn't make a pet.'

'I don' want a pet. I can't 'ave a pet,' he said, shaking his head as the tears, now flowing freely, ran down his face. 'They won' let me have a dog nor a cat nor nothin' – but I could have had the h'owl an' kept him in the box an' they wouldn't 'ave known. We could 'ave been pals. An' you let 'im go!'

Then, shaking himself free, he turned and looked once more to the top of the pole.

'Goodbye, h'owl!' he shouted, then, rubbing his eyes with the sleeve of his jacket, before I could say anything ran off up the lane.

I must have been shattered by Percy's reaction because I was quite startled when a voice said:

'Mr Lasgarn!'

I turned to find a middle-aged lady leaning on an old-fashioned 'sit up and beg' bicycle standing behind me, having come from the direction of the church.

'It is Mr Lasgarn, is it not?' she enquired. 'I am Miss Larkins, I play the organ. The vicar said you and your family had come to live here and we all hope you'll be very happy.' Then she looked on up the lane to where Percy was just about to disappear out of sight.

'I lost his owl for him,' I said. 'He's awfully upset.'

'Well, you cannot be expected to cure everything,' she said, in a comforting tone.

'But I did cure it,' I said. 'That's why I lost it.'

Miss Larkins smiled serenely but quizzically, so I directed her gaze to the top of the pole and explained what had happened.

'He's not the only one who is upset, by the sound of it, Mr Lasgarn,' she said gently, when I had finished the tale. 'But I don't think it would have been a good thing for Percy to have kept it – not in the circumstances.'

'What circumstances?' I asked.

'Not a very happy home life,' she explained tactfully. 'Mother and father divorced – different partners. The new Mrs Bapton is very strict on the children, very strict indeed.'

'No pets,' I said.

'Too houseproud for that,' she added, raising her eyebrows. 'Now I've a little dog,' she continued, changing the subject. 'Real little scruff, but he's a jewel. Romps all over the house, but I wouldn't be without him for the world. When I get home now, he'll be dancing about as if I'd just returned from Australia, and he's always the same.'

'That's the nice thing about them,' I agreed.

'Very true, Mr Lasgarn.' She brushed down the folds of her coat and straightened up her bicycle ready for the off. 'Do you know what? The more I see of people, the more I like my dog!'

I remembered that my old landlady in Putsley used to subscribe to that maxim as well and she was a spinster and rode a bike, too. Then Miss Larkins hopped upon her iron steed, the proportions not dissimilar to the Little Owl atop the telegraph pole, and set off up the lane.

'Don't worry about Percy Bapton,' she called back. 'I've got something for him!'

Slightly mystified by her parting shot, I waved goodbye and turned my attention once more to the Little Owl. What was he thinking about? I wondered, up there on his pole, and was he aware of the upset he'd created? If he was he didn't show it.

I was about to go back into the surgery when Branston came along again. He looked up at the owl and barked. The owl pulled himself to his full height, which altogether was not very high, then cocked his head to one side indignantly.

Branston barked again and with that, having had enough of dogs and people, the owl took off in the direction of the church tower, standing some two hundred yards away, and disappeared through one of the stone inlets.

'Satisfied?' I asked Branston, who I really felt should accept some responsibility.

But, typical of a Jack Russell, he was convinced that everything he did was right, so there was no point in arguing with him – which is another reason, I suppose, why dogs are such good companions!

A week later Percy Bapton turned up again, with a pair of binoculars slung around his neck.

'I come to thank you for seein' to the h'owl,' he said. 'An' I don't mind now 'cos I got these.'

He held up his acquisition proudly.

'That's a fine pair of glasses,' I said. 'Where did they come from?'

'Miss Larkins what plays on the h'organ,' he explained. 'They was her Dad's, an' he used to watch the birds. An' Miss Larkins said it was better to watch them in their own

16

homes than keep them in ours. So that's what I'm going to do.'

What a kind and thoughtful person was Miss Larkins, I reflected.

'He flew away then,' said Percy, directing his glasses at the top of the pole.

'He went into the church tower,' I said, 'shortly after you left.'

'Do you think I could see him?' said Percy, training the glasses onto the stonework.

'I doubt it,' I said. 'He probably wouldn't have stayed there.'

Percy scanned the tower for some time, holding the glasses very professionally with straightened palms at either side, in the manner of a ship's captain on the bridge.

Then he let out a shriek of delight: 'There 'e is!' he yelled. 'There's our little h'owl!'

He passed the glasses to me and I focused on the stonework and the inlet through which I had watched him disappear. Sure enough, perched just within the recess, half-hidden by shadow, was a small feathered creature, its eyes crystal-bright even from that distance.

Of course it might not have been the same one, though the quaint way it cocked its head now and again made me feel it was.

'Can I come down an' look at him when I want?' said Percy.

'You do that,' I told him. Not that I had any jurisdiction over who looked at the church, but it was nice of him to ask.

'I can keep an eye on him, then,' said Percy.

'And he can keep an eye on you, too,' I reminded him.

'And you!' he chirped. 'He's right by your house. He'll be able to see everything you do.'

'That's very true, Percy,' I said.

And as I watched him earnestly studying the owl through his glasses, I wondered indeed what sort of goings-on our mutual feathered friend would be party to, in and around Gatewood, Welbury, during the coming months.

2

If Percy Bapton's 'h'owl' had a good view of the centre of the village, to appreciate it in its entirety one had to journey to Scrambletop, a ridge some five hundred feet high that extended for two miles to the south-east. From the point looking towards Welbury it turned almost at right angles, gently sloping away directly west until it blended with the farmland around Mansel Gracey.

The road to the ridge wound its way through a pine-wood, with seemingly endless grassy rides leading off at intervals. The wood itself was dense, secretive, and when the wicked Welsh mists sneaked down the valley and shrouded the higher ground, even sinister.

But on a clear day, once past the tree-line, the tightly packed firs gave way to a patch of common land from which the view was truly breathtaking. It was said that seven counties could be seen when the visibility was perfect; but if that was doubtful one thing was certain, and that was the richness and undeniable beauty of the immediate countryside below, with Welbury nestling in its folds.

For miles around the eye was treated to a veritable panorama of all that was good in agriculture: red cattle against a lush green back-cloth, speckle-faced sheep, orchards, hopyards and golden waving corn in season.

Such was the view and such was the balance of farming twenty years ago, though patterns and policies change and things are not what they used to be; yet rural bliss was not all-pervading even in those days, as I discovered on my first visit to Alwyn Blake's few acres, set amid the high woodland – and the view I experienced on that day was far from beautiful.

Pridewell possessed a rather Tyrolean atmosphere: the

farmstead positioned amid the pines, the timbered structure and wide, sweeping gables of the house and buildings adding to the impression.

Alwyn and his wife were a diligent pair, having come to Pridewell from Wales with the hopeful intention of using it as a stepping-stone to bigger things. It was a tidy holding, with well-kept gates and hedges, healthy pastures and flourishing livestock; for although the acreage was small, the quality of the animals and crops was second to none. There were twenty-seven grand Hereford cattle of good pedigree, Alwyn having bought them in, not cheaply but with sound judgement to establish the basis of a future, larger enterprise.

Deep litter hens, two Large White sows and progeny, a Jersey house cow and fifty Clun ewes made up the rest of the stock.

Alwyn was 'Welsh-built', stocky and strong with a deep, rich voice that in song readily enhanced the choral works of the church choir; but his voice on the phone the morning he rang was weak, faltering and that of a broken man.

'Come an' see my sheep, please!'

It was almost a plea, more childlike than that one might expect from a grown man.

'Don' know if you can do anything – too late for most of 'em – too late . . .'

His voice became faint again and I probed gently for further explanation.

'What's happened?' I asked.

'Happened . . . what's happened?' he sounded in a daze, then I heard him draw a deep breath. 'Dogs!' he blurted. 'They've been run by dogs!' I heard him sigh again.

'I'll come now,' I said, but Alwyn had already put down the phone.

It was a blustery morning as I drove to Scrambletop; there was rain in the air but it was coming to little, giving the windscreen wipers only half a job to do.

Higher up the hill the wind became more boisterous, and though the close-packed pines gave little indication of

19

its strength, once I reached the more exposed common land I felt my car lifting on its springs as the sharp gusts cut beneath.

Just at the junction where the farm lane began, I noticed the meadow gate was open and, looking across the field, could see in the distance some vehicles with figures gathered near. One of the trucks was a green Morris pick-up which I knew to be Alwyn's; so leaving the road, I drove across the field towards it.

There were five men in all, besides Alwyn: Will Barlow and his son who farmed Watton at the bottom of the hill; Reg Phelps, a forester with the Commission, and two others I did not know.

They were standing with their backs to me, near a gate in the corner of the field – but this one was closed. And when the men parted and turned at my arrival I caught sight of what they were looking at.

It was a sickening mound of dead animals.

They said nothing as I got out of the car – not even Alwyn. They just looked at me, then turned back to the macabre sodden heap.

That they were sheep was straightforward to ascertain, but as to individuals, it was impossible to tell, for they were so entwined – a conglomeration of legs and fleece – yet hardly any heads were visible. Initially the grotesque scene seemed unbelievable, then logic prevailed and it became clear that the structure of the carnage had been caused by hysterical panic, terminating in shock and suffocation.

Alwyn looked across to me, then shook his head.

'Over forty of 'em – dead as doornails.'

'No survivors,' I confirmed.

'Seven, down at the farm. They must have split from the main bunch – Reg found 'em in the wood. This lot tried to get away through the gate, poor sods; but it wouldn't give – one of the penalties for hanging 'em well,' he said with a wry smile.

I could imagine the chase: the pounding of hooves, the bleating, the weaving and checking – then the run for the gate. The leaders banging against it, attempting to push through the bars; the followers piling in on top, burying their heads in the seething, steaming mass of bodies, desperate in a futile search for escape.

'No sign of the dog,' I said.

'Dogs,' said Alwyn. 'Two of the bastards. A Black Labrador and a rough coated terrier, small dog – like a Jack Russell. Yes, Will's boy saw 'em running across their ground just on first light.'

The boy nodded. 'Fair way off they were,' he said, 'but they must have been the ones.'

'Any insurance cover, Alwyn?'

He shook his head. 'Dead loss, unless we get the owner.'

'There's a lot of dogs like them about,' said Will Barlow. 'P'raps Bob knows,' as through the gate and across the field trundled the little black A35 of PC Packham.

'Didn't fancy biking it up here,' he puffed, as he extracted his ample form from the small saloon. 'Oh, my God!' he exclaimed, as his eye met the sheep. 'Poor devils! How many, Alwyn?'

'Best part of forty,' came the sad reply. 'Might as well have had the bloody lot!'

'Sorry, I am,' said Bob, with genuine sincerity. 'You could have done without this, boy,' he put his hand on Alwyn's shoulder. 'I'll see if I can't run 'em down.'

'I'll pop over the farm and check those others,' I offered. Alwyn nodded.

'I will need to have a word with you before you go, Mr Lasgarn,' said Bob Packham, unfolding his notebook. 'Official cause of death an' that – not that it takes much reasoning, beg your pardon.' He gave a low whistle. 'Then, we'll make a few enquiries!'

Down at the farm I met Mrs Blake, looking as shattered as her husband. She showed me the remaining sheep in a pen and helped me catch them for examination.

Four had distinct signs of congestion of the lungs precipitated by exhaustion; I treated them with penicillin to counteract any secondary pneumonia and also gave them an injection to combat the shock. Then, declining a cup of tea from Mrs Blake, I returned to the field.

The men and vehicles were now at the top of the lane, Bob Packham having got all his details sorted out.

I explained my treatment of the survivors to Alwyn and said I would call the following day to check upon their condition.

'Perhaps I could have a certificate from you, Mr Lasgarn, stating what you've seen. Just in case we ever get anyone for it.'

'You don't sound too hopeful,' I said.

PC Packham re-buttoned the top of his tunic which he had undone on arriving at the scene. 'The burden of guilt, Mr Lasgarn, is not easy to apportion,' he replied, in a judicial tone. 'They are not all like Sam Juggins' case.'

His comment took me back to my very first involvement with sheep worrying back in Ledingford, shortly after I joined the Hacker practice.

Sam Juggins was a likeable old rascal who farmed near Ledingford and was as sharp as they came, but good-hearted with it. His collie dog, Snapper, had been accused of killing a neighbour's lamb, and I had resorted to an old trick I had learnt when seeing practice in Newpool with C. J. Pink. Snapper was given a lump of washing soda, following which he brought up the remains of a meal consisting not of lamb, but rabbit! Snapper was exonerated and Sam became my friend for life.

'That was justice,' I said, 'but we had a suspect then.'

'That we did,' said Bob. 'This pair could be well away by now.' He rubbed his stubbly chin, no doubt having missed his morning shave in the urgency to come to Pridewell. 'Only justice for these devils is a dose of lead shot, when they do it again.'

'They'll get that all right if they come back here,' said Alwyn. 'Not that there's that much to come back for.'

'They'll do it somewhere,' said Bob. 'Can't leave it alone once they've started.'

With that, we dispersed and as I drove back I did not

see the view, for the sight of that heartbreaking pile of Alwyn's dead sheep saturated my thoughts.

The rest of the day, fortunately, was busy, giving me no time to dwell on the morning's happenings.

Being Autumn, many dairy cows were calving, their pregnancies arranged to produce winter milk, which was more profitable than the summer supply.

Indeed, the dairy cow was a considerable source of work and income to any veterinary practice; for apart from the complications at the actual birth, there were such associated ailments as retention of foetal membranes, prolapses, milk fever, mastitis and suchlike, which needed attention.

In fact, pregnancy and its manifestations were to a great extent what stockfarming was all about; but as for complications, there were some rather more subtle than the obvious – as I had only recently learned at a dinner party at John Carpenter's.

I had become friendly with John ever since the day I first arrived at his place to treat a case of 'foul' of the foot in one of his Friesians. It was milking time and the cow wasn't ready, so he gave me his twelve-bore with some cartridges and suggested I went rough shooting for an hour.

It was an unexpected gesture and I thoroughly enjoyed the stroll; since then I often went over on a Saturday afternoon in the season and found the sport both exhilarating and yet relaxing.

He would lend me his dog, Jess, a beautifully gentle Golden Retriever with a mouth as soft as silk. Yet despite her calm temperament, she was magic when it came to finding a fallen bird. I would dearly have liked a pup from her and once asked John whether he had ever contemplated letting his bitch have a litter.

'She's far too precious,' he told me, ruffling Jess's coat affectionately. 'I wouldn't want to put her through all that pain.'

At the dinner party some time later I was seated next to

his wife; we got to talking about dogs and I happened to mention what a super dog was Jess.

And then I told John's wife why he wouldn't let Jess have pups.

She went practically purple; 'So that's what he said, did he?' she fumed. 'Far too precious, is she? And I gave him five kids without so much as a murmur!'

She shot a glance across the table to where John was busily chatting up Diana. He smiled congenially, blissfully unaware of the mire into which he had just been deposited by my untimely remarks.

Fortunately both Di and I were well away by the time he was!

* * *

As the majority of our clients in the area were farmers, I had not initially developed any facilities for the handling of domestic pets, not having foreseen much demand in that direction.

It was an aspect I had underestimated, as there was a considerable dog and cat population both in the village and in the surrounding countryside; and so I decided to convert a small store-room at the side of the house into a mini-surgery.

On the evening after visiting Pridewell I was busy priming the walls of my new development, when Diana came in to say there was a call.

'It's a Mrs Gooding,' she said, 'very upset – her dog has been in an accident. She's a widow,' Di continued, 'lives at Myrtle Cottage just past the school. Nice old lady, I met her in the Post Office yesterday.'

In fact Diana had learnt more about local folks than I had in the short time we had been in Welbury, which was a great help when it came to visits.

'I'll go,' I said, 'and you can finish this for me, if you like.'

'There's enough paint on you to give it another coat,' she chided, taking the brush. 'Hugh. What a mess!'

True, I was not the handiest of men around the house, as a picture in the hallway signified. It was about four feet across and eighteen inches high, depicting a Dutch carnival scene. Diana had admired it in Ledingford some time previously and I had bought it as a surprise when we moved in. She was thrilled, and after decorating the hallway and staircase, decided exactly where she would like it hung.

So it was that, one afternoon when she was out, I decided to carry out the job, and set to with a happy heart. I measured distance from four directions, allowed for slackness in the wire and the level of the wall, taking absolute care with every move I made. With the precision of a brain surgeon, I commenced to hammer in the especially strengthened nail, tap by cautious tap.

At the third blow, a small piece of plaster about the size of a shilling fell away from the base of the nail, but unperturbed I hammered on. Two more blows and a larger portion about three inches across came adrift and floated to the floor. There was now quite a hole, but as it would be covered by the picture, anyway, I continued.

I was within a millimetre of the required position and had delivered the final tap, when it happened. As if by magic, accompanied by a crack like lightning, the whole wall suddenly became restructured into a mozaic pattern of fractured plaster – from ceiling to skirting board!

I stood back for a moment in absolute disbelief.

Yet before I could blink, the pieces fell from the wall one by one, and as they clattered to the floor I became enveloped in a cloud of white dust. Coughing and spluttering, I stepped backwards, only to put my foot through the glass of the picture which I had laid 'carefully' on the floor out of harm's way!

Following Di's reaction on her return, I firmly resolved never to undertake any more household jobs than were absolutely necessary!

Myrtle Cottage was the last house on the Mansel Gracey road out of the village; it was typical of so many of the Tudor dwellings in the area, and as I pushed open the wooden gate and surveyed its ancient timbers and peeling plaster, with my 'do-it-yourself' reminiscences still fresh in my mind, I was glad I was coming to see a dog and not hang a picture.

Mrs Gooding was indeed a sweet old lady and the inside of her home was warm and cosy. She invited me into the living-room and explained what had happened.

'So kind of you to come straight away,' she said. 'Though fortunately it's not a desperate emergency, thank goodness.'

She motioned me to sit down and took an armchair opposite.

'Bobby was really my late husband's dog,' she said. 'Sadly, Charles passed away last June,' she pointed to a photograph of a military looking gentleman on the mantel-shelf. 'Oh, they were such wonderful pals.' Her pale eyes lit up with happiness at the memories. 'They would go for miles in the countryside together. Charles and Bobby knew every inch of it around here. I couldn't go because of my arthritis – but those two . . . ' she paused again as her thoughts took over. 'My grief at Charlie's passing was helped by the knowledge of what had happened – heart attack, you know – he didn't suffer. But Bobby, how could he understand? I worried that he might have felt deserted; feel that Charles had abandoned him, and in fact, for ages Bobby just lay around like a lifeless thing. Then, three weeks ago, he became quite naughty and started breaking out of the garden, and that's how he came to be involved in an accident. I'll go and get him.'

She rose and went to a door covered by an orange-patterned curtain which she drew aside slightly, then opened it.

'Come on, Bobby darling,' she called. 'Mr Lasgarn's come to make you better.'

I heard a slight scuffle followed by a whine, and Bobby appeared.

Immediately I noticed the dried blood on his chest and the mud sticking to his thick coat; but the factor that disturbed me most was not his possible injuries, for they did not appear too severe, it was his breed. Bobby was a Black Labrador!

He came towards me in a friendly fashion, but halted just out of my reach, as if slightly uncertain of my intentions. Then he turned back to Mrs Gooding and sat down by her side.

A Black Labrador, on the loose, his coat covered in mud and blood; a Black Labrador that knew every inch of the countryside around Welbury.

My heart sank as I began to think of the possible consequences of my visit. If it was Bobby that had been involved in the running of Alwyn Blake's flock, Mrs Gooding would be held responsible and liable to pay compensation which could run to a considerable sum of money; but more tragic would be having to put Bobby down, for a reprieve following such a horrific attack would be out of the question.

Mrs Gooding was chatting away, but I did not absorb a thing she was saying, for I was trying desperately to think how I could avoid reporting the incident that could well break an old lady's heart, and at the same time be fair to Alwyn Blake.

Leaving my chair, I knelt in front of Bobby and ran my hands over him.

He had a small cut about half an inch in length on his right foreleg, a deeper one on his chest and a graze beneath his right eye; but none of the injuries were sufficient to account for the amount of blood on his coat.

However, when I reflected his lips and opened his mouth I discovered he had bitten his tongue, deeply and at some length; that, I knew, could produce a considerable degree of haemorrhage, especially if he had attempted to clean the other wounds at the same time.

'What was the accident?' I asked Mrs Gooding, trying not to make my enquiry sound like an interrogation.

'I don't really know,' she said, 'but it must have been a car, mustn't it?'

Must it? I thought.

'There has been some sheep worrying up at Pridewell,' I said. 'They are looking for a . . .'

Mrs Gooding raised her hands in shock.

'Oh! Mr Lasgarn! Bobby wouldn't do that! What a thought. He is far too gentle to upset anything. Charlie used to say that whenever they were up that way, he never so much as looked at a sheep!'

It was a pretty positive defence, but now she had told me the dog did have knowledge of that particular area, which was another damning factor.

I looked at Bobby, and with his big brown eyes he blinked innocently back at me.

'Where were you on the night of the twenty-fifth? Can you prove it? Have you got an alibi?'

'Of course I can prove it. I was with my girl-friend in Mansel Gracey – spent the night there. You know how it is,' he winked knowingly. 'Then her husband came home unexpectedly, bit of a punch-up and I left – worth it, though!'

He stood up and wagged his tail – and I believed him!

If only they could talk!

I treated his wounds and reassured Mrs Gooding that his injuries would soon heal and, as far as I could ascertain, there should be no complications.

'You don't know what Bobby means to me now that Charlie's gone, Mr Lasgarn,' she said as I was leaving.

That was the thing – I did. And it was that very fact that was on my mind when I arrived back at Gatewood.

Diana had finished painting and was making some cocoa.

'How's the dog?' she asked.

'All I hope is he did go to Mansel Gracey to see his girl,' I said, wearily.

Diana turned, cup in hand: 'Who went to Mansel Gracey?'

'Bobby!'

'Bobby who . . . ?'

So I told her all about the case, my suspicions and my dilemma.

28

'Poor Mrs Gooding,' said Di, when I had finished.

'Poor Alwyn Blake and his forty-odd dead sheep,' I added.

She put her arm around me. 'What are you going to do, Hugh?'

'Well, it is only circumstantial, but as PC Packham said, if it is Bobby, he'll do it again – and then the obvious thing to ask is, why wasn't he reported the first time? And if it's known that I saw him and kept quiet about it, I'm not going to be very popular in agricultural circles, am I!'

'Isn't it against your code to do that sort of thing?' she said.

'Well, one doesn't normally talk about cases, as you know; but if a dog is a killer, there is an obligation.'

'Come on, darling, don't try and work it out tonight, sleep on it,' she said sympathetically.

But though I agreed, I was fully aware that the decision would still be there the following morning.

The fact that after a disturbed night I had reached no firm conclusion created in me a mild panic when PC Packham turned up on my doorstep at eight o'clock that morning.

'You wouldn't happen to have treated a Black Labrador covered in blood recently, Mr Lasgarn?' he asked, his tone sounding rather accusing, as if he suspected I was trying to cover it up.

'Yes. I did,' I admitted, but refrained from giving any further detail,

'When was that?' he glanced down at his notebook.

'Last night.'

'About what time?'

'Eight o'clock – or just after.'

Then he looked me straight in the eyes and asked: 'Where?'

It was no good hedging, so I told him exactly what I had seen and that my patient was Mrs Gooding's dog, Bobby.

When I had finished, the constable consulted his notebook once more.

'It fits, by the look of it,' he said. 'That'll be him!'

'It's only circumstantial!' I said, rather sharply. 'No definite proof!'

'True,' he said. 'True. But Mrs Gooding does live out on the Mansel Gracey road and the chap who ran in to him said it was definitely a Black Labrador.'

'Car accident!' I stuttered.

'Yes,' he replied. 'Bank manager from Ledingford. Very upset he was, too, said he never saw him. Black dog on a dark night, understandable, I suppose. Anyway, he said to send him the bill for any treatment, which was decent, for I know for a fact that little Mrs Gooding isn't too well britched.'

'That's good news!' I said. 'I did wonder . . .'

'Alwyn's sheep?'

'Yes.'

'Will Barlow shot the two of 'em this morning. Tried to run his flock and he got both!' He slid his notebook back into his tunic pocket. 'I'm just off down to get the facts, ought to be able to trace one of 'em, at least!'

With an unbelievable sigh of relief, I went back inside.

'You told him,' said Di.

I nodded.

'Bobby did go to see his girl-friend after all,' I said.

'Naughty boy!' said Di.

'Well at least you don't get shot for it!'

'Don't be so sure!' she said with a laugh. 'Come and have your breakfast.'

And feeling very relieved that the problem had been solved, I did just that.

3

I completed my conversion of the store-room into a mini-surgery by installing a low suite kitchen cabinet, a relic of the practice house in Ledingford, to house instruments; together with the redundant examination table from the 'exotic plant' consulting room at St Mark's Square and some shelves for drug bottles and pill containers.

The exposed timbers I covered with a false plasterboard ceiling; coated the primed brick walls with snow-white emulsion and even fixed up a rudimentary examination light by rewiring part of the electrical circuit – something of which I was rather proud, considering the limits of my DIY potential. Though I said it myself, it was a tidy job – small, but efficiently furbished and enough to satisfy the foreseeable requirements.

On the Saturday afternoon my new conception was complete; and on the Sunday, after lunch, it was christened – though not as I might have wished!

A Mr Mabbit, who described himself as an ''orticulturist' from Bedwardine, rang in a very distressed state, saying his Irish Setter, Mitch, had jumped over a wall onto a garden cloche. The glass frame had shattered, badly cutting the dog's leg.

I told Mr Mabbit to come over straight away and went enthusiastically into my brand-new facility to make things ready.

Within half an hour, a small blue van pulled up outside and from the back emerged a small man – Mr Mabbit the ''orticulturist' – cradling the unfortunate Mitch. He staggered into my new premises and deposited the dog upon the table. It was easy to see the considerable gash on the left hind limb and though it had bled profusely, the flow

31

had been sensibly stemmed by the application of a hand-kerchief in the form of a tourniquet, above the hock.

'Lovely dog 'e is,' gasped Mr Mabbit, 'but a might flighty when 'e's frightened.'

The setter lay in a remarkably composed manner upon the table, in contrast to its owner who, to say the least, was considerably agitated. It was obvious that the wound would need several stitches and in order to examine it more thoroughly I took the oval switch of my self-installed examination light in my hand.

'Let's brighten things up,' I said to Mr Mabbit with a confident smile – and so saying, I pressed the switch.

I don't think, if I was a TV panellist with a chance of a trip to Mars, I could have guessed what would happen next, for the sequence of events was so rapid that it defied categorizing.

The second my thumb depressed the black plastic switch – the bulb exploded. Not just a pop, but an almighty BANG! Splinters of glass showered upon us and the room filled with grey smoke, accompanied by the fishy aroma of burnt electrical fittings.

I had obviously got my wires crossed!

With a piercing howl Mitch leaped from the table and crashed headlong into the erstwhile kitchen cabinet, caus-ing the doors to fly open and discharge the instruments on top of him.

This only served to upset the poor creature even more, and in an attempt to climb the wall, the handkerchief tourniquet fell off and blood spurted in all directions like water from a demented hosepipe – except that it was red, sticky and went all over in wavy stripes!

The dimensions of the mini-surgery were such that although adequate for client, patient and vet, it was assumed that both humans would stand in an orderly fashion by the table, with the patient to be treated lying quietly on top. But a 'bleeding' setter – and I use the word in its fullest sense – on the rampage threw everything out of proportion. Between my legs, under the table, up the wall – the haemorrhagic canine was everywhere and all the time spouting red: over my coat, Mr Mabbit's trousers, the floor, the table and, most harrowing of all, my virgin-white, newly painted wall.

Eventually I collared the dog and managed to calm it down. Then, dusting away the glass with my sleeve, I lifted it back onto the table where it lay shivering and exhausted, enabling me to re-apply the tourniquet.

'Perhaps now we can get something done,' I said, looking at Mr Mabbit, but he had turned cabbage green and was furiously tugging at his collar. Before I could say: 'Are you all right?' he keeled over sideways like a felled spruce and as he did so, his hand reached out, grabbing the top shelf of my newly erected drug display.

Mr Mabbit went down, the shelf went down, and a cascade of bottles and pill containers followed, some discharging their contents in a psychedelic hailstorm.

For the second time, and not without reason, Mitch leapt hysterically to his feet, but this time I hung on and, in competition with his howling, yelled as loudly as I could: 'DIANA!'

She came almost immediately and, assessing the situation instantly, half dragged, half fireman-lifted little Mr Mabbit off to the kitchen.

'I'll make him some sweet tea,' she said. 'His wife is in the car, I had better get her.'

I told Mitch to stay put on the table, which, surprisingly enough, he did, obviously deciding that in such crazy circumstances it was most probably the safest place. My intention was to make up a sedative injection for him before I commenced my suturing – although I was nearly on the verge of needing one myself.

As I retrieved the appropriate bottle from the pile at my feet, the door opened and an exceedingly large lady appeared. She wore a voluminous flower-print dress, and her face was very round and red, with straggling hair topped by a blue beret. Yet for all her size, from her smile she looked a jolly woman, which in the circumstances I deemed to be an excellent thing.

'I'm Tom's wife. Oh, I am sorry about him, m'dear,' she

33

said, shaking her head. 'No stomach for that sort of thing. I told 'im I should have brought Mitchy in the first place. But no, he wouldn't have it. What a man!' She squeezed past me to a position nearer Mitch's head and stroked him. 'Don't worry, pet. Mother's 'ere now,' she cooed.

'It is a bit claustrophobic in here,' I admitted, 'and with the chasing about and the blood, Mr Mabbit's reaction was quite understandable.' I fitted the needle to the syringe of sedative. 'Now I'm going to give this to Mitch to relax him,' I explained. 'Then, with some local anaesthetic infiltrated around the wound area, I can start suturing. I expect it will need at least a dozen stitches, so if you would like to stay at the head and comfort him, I'll see to the rest.'

She nodded her agreement and, after picking up some of the bottles underfoot and scuffing the rest beneath the table, I set to the task.

Mrs Mabbit was indeed of considerable proportions, and though she was at the front of the dog and I was working at the rear, her ample form kept encroaching upon my section of the table, obstructing what light there was; on two occasions when she leaned forward to take a closer look at what I was doing, my left elbow inadvertently jabbed her in mid-bosom, to which she giggled, 'Ooh! Sooory, m'dear!'

However, the anaesthetic had taken well and the surgical repair progressed smoothly.

The upper and lower limits of the wound were straight-forward skin closures, for the glass had split the tissue as deftly as a surgical knife; but at the centre the damage was deeper, having lacerated the tendon, which demanded some rather more detailed work.

Eventually I completed that part of the restoration and was about to rethread my needle when I became conscious of a rushing sound and felt the pressure of a warm draught upon my neck.

Such had been my concentration upon the job in hand that I had completely forgotten about Mrs Mabbit, and to my horror, when I looked up I saw she was about to faint as well!

The rushing wind was her accelerated breathing, which was soon accompanied by a low moaning sound; her eyes glazed and, with arms raised, like a collapsing chimney stack she fell towards me.

I put out my hands, partly in an attempt to arrest her fall, but also to shield myself from major injury. Realizing only just in time that I held a very sharp needle in my right hand, and in a frantic move to discard it, I left myself vulnerable to the full force of her body. Her arms dropped around my neck and over she came, like a giant hippo flopping into a river.

Never in the darkest depths of the roughest, sweatiest rugby scrum – and I had been in a few – had I experienced such terror, as she flattened me to the floor, head smothered in her gigantic chest. No way could I even gasp 'DIANA!' who was ministering to my captor's husband in the kitchen.

Dead weight she was and out stone cold, her arms enfolding me in a wrestler's embrace.

Thankfully – and miraculously – Diana did come to the rescue, and although she cracked me on the head when she opened the door, I was never more grateful for an intrusion.

Mrs Mabbit eventually recovered and while Di fed hot sweet tea to her, as well as her husband, I completed the repair on Mitch, who by now was spark out from the injection.

It took until eight o'clock that evening to clean and restructure the room.

I rewired the examination light in the correct manner and replaced the shelving, again making good another mistake which had contributed to its detachment: my Rawlplug screws into the wall had in several instances gone alongside the fillers instead of through them.

As I finally sank into my armchair, I realized it would be

necessary to improve the ventilation if I was to avoid further catastrophes of a similar nature.

Diana came through with some cocoa.

'Thanks for your help,' I said. 'Animals I can manage – people are the problem!' She smiled and sat down at my feet. 'Lucky you came when you did, darling. How did you know what was going on?'

Diana took a drink from her mug, then laid her head back upon my knees.

'Feminine intuition, Mr Lasgarn,' she said with a chuckle. 'A wife always knows when her husband is playing around with another woman.'

* * *

The mini-surgery proved a great success and my 'small animal' clients increased in number. I was very happy with the situation and began to find the treatment of pets, together with sporting animals such as gundogs, ferrets and foxhounds, just as absorbing as farm practice, though the latter was still the main source of my work.

Yet it was in the surgery that I was getting the feel of the environment, each client and animal encapsulating a piece of local atmosphere in a manner I had not experienced in the town practice of Ledingford.

They seemed more individual, not only in dress and character, but even in their origins, for not all were true locals, many having retired to the village and its surroundings. Such folk had plenty of time to care for and spend upon their pets, which were very much a part of their existence, and I began more and more to realize the value of companion animals in society.

All this and living now, as well as working, in the countryside, made me begin to feel very much a part of the Borders, and although I could never sever my Welsh roots, or would ever want to, I was beginning to perceive that my transplantation into Herefordshire was becoming permanent.

Yet if a sense of belonging was being engendered by our

move to Welbury, there were certain enigmas about country life that were now coming to light.

Firstly, there was the association with the supposedly 'upright' and those that were not so. Although to me all men through their animals were equal, it did not always work that way in the countryside, and I often found myself, to use an appropriate phrase for a vet, running with the hare and hunting with the hounds.

Take the case of the Smiths, whom I first encountered close on midnight, when they came to my door with a lurcher on a string.

The fact that it was well after surgery hours and I was clad in pyjamas seemed to worry them not at all, for they just fingered the edge of their black greasy locks in a fleeting salute of respect, then the shorter of the two said:

'Could you look at me dog, sir? Been bit bad, 'e has.'

'Do you know what time it is?' I asked sharply as the aroma of woodsmoke drifted around me. The gypsies looked at each other in mild surprise, as if time was hardly relevant.

'When did it happen?' I continued.

'A while back,' came the non-committal reply.

''Tis me little girl's dog,' said the one holding the string, 'and if anything happened to 'er dog, that little child would die of sorrow, sir.'

He looked at me appealingly, and despite the fact that it was obviously a bit of 'diddy-coi' eyewash, I found myself relenting.

'Where is it?' I asked.

'It's 'is stopper, sir. Got bit on 'is stopper.'

Now stoppers I did know about, although I had not had occasion to treat one since qualifying; but when I was a student seeing practice in Newpool with C. J. Pink, MRCVS, their treatment was a common occurrence.

The stopper is rudimentary and a termination of the accessory carpal bone; in anatomical parlance it is situated medial and distal to the accessory carpal bone. The meta-podio-phalangeal joint rests upon it when the paw sup-ports the weight.

Fundamentally it is known to the veterinary anatomists as *Torus metacarpalis*, though to the Smiths and to many other afficianados of the dogtrack, it is a stopper – just as simple as that.

The importance to each calling varied infinitely: to the purist it was an evolutionary indicator in the regression of five-toed carnivores; to the Taff, it was equivalent to an aerofoil brake and cash in hand.

The veterinary problems at Newpool concerned 'scrubbing'.

They occurred invariably on the racetrack or during hare coursing, when the dog stopped short and the 'wrists' would sink like the springs on a car chassis and act as a brake pad.

This assisted the arrest, but on occasions, if the pace was fierce and the halt sudden, the stopper could be 'scrubbed' or grazed on the ash track or hard ground and in some cases even knocked off.

The latter was a minor disaster for, apart from the inability to add to the braking power, its absence tended to throw the dog off balance when cornering: so preservation of the stopper was essential and needed immediate attention.

Amidst profuse gratitude involving my instant beatification to a 'saint' and a more realistic compliment that I was a 'proper gentleman and good fortune would surely come my way', I led the nocturnal trio into the surgery.

It was at that point that they announced they were the Smith brothers, Dan and Nathan, and that the lurcher was called Sprat.

Whilst apparel in operating theatres is not dissimilar to some forms of night attire, I felt my red stripe St Michaels to be somewhat inappropriate and covered up with a white coat.

It was a typical 'scrub', the pad having been lifted from its attachment, which was now just a flap, hanging by barely a thread of tissue.

'It's as good as off,' I told them, putting down the lurcher's leg.

'Save it if you can, for me child's sake,' pleaded Dan. 'Think of the heartbreak for the little mite if her dog lost 'is stopper.'

'Dog bit it, you say?' I eyed the two suspiciously.

They both nodded, but didn't raise their eyes.

'I know about stoppers,' I said, 'and this has been "scrubbed".'

At the mention of such a knowledgeable term, they both looked up.

'Now I don't want to know where, but I would like to know how,' I continued. 'There are no flapping tracks in this part of the world.'

They looked at each other and I could sense the consternation in their minds.

'Lamping?' I asked.

That made them both start and they looked nervously around as if expecting to see PC Packham standing behind them; then finding he was not, admitted the cause with sheepish nods.

'Good,' I said. 'That part doesn't worry me, but if it is a genuine scrub I can probably save it – if it's a bite, then I can't.'

Lamping is much used amongst the poaching fraternity and involves shining a beam to dazzle the game. Birds will sit, but hares and rabbits run for their lives down the shaft of light with the dog in hot pursuit, skidding to a halt at the catch.

This, I surmised, was how Sprat's injury had occurred, a fact which was confirmed by Nathan.

'Yes sir, it is a "scrub",' he said, 'an' me an' Dan is very grateful for your understandin'.'

For the next hour I repaired the wound.

The task was more complicated than it appeared, for pad tissue is very fragile and sutures do not hold well; yet it is vitally important to get firm adhesion of the healing surfaces, so that both internal and external suturing is necessary.

When the work was completed and the leg bandaged, I gave instructions about aftercare, to which both listened attentively. They paid on the spot from a great roll of notes Dan took from his hip pocket – which made my fee look very reasonable.

Whether they thought so too, I did not know, but shortly after they had disappeared into the night and I was cleaning up, there came another tap at the door. It was Nathan who, before I could say anything, thrust a brace of still warm pheasant into my hand and said:

'For you and your family.'

Then he disappeared again.

A few days later, Colonel Bracegirdle brought his Labrador, Skipper, for a vaccination, and complained heatedly about the recent spate of poaching and how the offenders should be punished – his suggestions being rather more drastic than the law allowed.

'Reckon the damn' rascals have taken over three hundred birds this season,' he fumed. 'What d'ye think of that, Lasgarn?'

I offered some sympathetic comment, but little did he know that my thoughts were really on the bottle of wine I intended to buy, to accompany a rather special meal that Di and myself were going to enjoy that evening.

* * *

If the enigma of the hare and the hounds was of significance in that case, it was an even more appropriate analogy when one became involved with truly wild creatures. The dilemma that every vet must face, at one time or another in the course of general practice, first came noticeably to me in a large, high-sided cardboard box.

It was early spring, and we had taken the girls for a day trip to the sea, returning to find the container deposited outside the surgery door. It was pretty obvious it was intended for my attention, but I approached it warily for I could see it was not a postal delivery, neither was there any note attached to give an indication of who had left it or of its contents.

Cautiously I raised the flaps, but as soon as I did so, a frantic scuffling and spitting from within caused me to close them quickly. Whatever was inside was either very frightened, vicious or both.

I carried the box into the surgery, the inmate banging about with such vigour that the box jumped uncannily on the table top.

Grabbing a metal grid I used to partition my large cat basket, and holding the box firmly, I slid it under the flaps and, with that security screen installed, was able to open up and peer inside.

Two bright, beady eyes met mine. A small nose twitched, whiskers quivered, sharp claws rattled on the cardboard, and with a swish of its furry tail a little grey squirrel set off on a frantic chase around the box.

When finally it ran out of steam and settled, I could see that it held one of its hind legs rather awkwardly, the injured limb no doubt being why the little creature had been brought to my door. Donning my trusty old leather 'cat gloves', which bore the scars of many a battle, I gingerly lowered my hand into the depths of the box. I held still for a few seconds, the squirrel suddenly froze and I swiftly caught it over the shoulders and lifted it out.

To my surprise it remained motionless, though I could feel its tiny heart thumping violently between my fingers. As I gently extended the injured limb, the little creature tensed and I realized that it had a broken leg.

It was remarkable that the squirrel had allowed me to make my examination without any struggle, and I eased my grip on the slim body – but in a flash it wriggled forward, turned its glossy head and bit right through the glove and into my finger.

Dancing with pain and loudly expressing my disapproval of its action, I deposited the squirrel back inside the box, whence it stared up at me with a distinctly apprehensive look on its face.

I inspected my injury which fortunately was not as severe as it might have been, the needle-sharp incisors having pierced just the edge of the flesh. The unexpected

41

and ungrateful reaction had peeved me considerably and, coupled with the fact that he was a pest with a broken leg, there would have been ample justification for solving the whole problem by swiftly finishing him off.

I opened the box again and he made to sit up, but fell to one side in obvious distress; twice more he tried before he eventually gave up and, exhausted, lay down on his side.

'Someone must care for you,' I said, 'or they wouldn't have brought you here. And as for biting me . . .' Well it really was my own fault, for who wouldn't react if a broken bone was disturbed, even in the cause of a diagnosis! Maybe the little fellow had taught me a lesson about complacency in handling my patients, about which I myself should be grateful; for that reason alone, I felt I owed him a favour.

'But if I'm going to help you, you're going to sleep first,' I told him.

There had recently been introduced a new sedative for cats, intramuscular and of small dosage; it was not licensed for squirrels, but I did not think the niceties of pharmaceutical legislation would concern my chap under the circumstances.

I computed the dose according to his size, and when I grabbed him for the second time I held him firmly; within minutes of giving the shot, he became lifeless.

For a long time there was no apparent respiration and I thought I had lost him, then I noticed a slight disturbance amongst the hairs on his chest and he started to breathe. I waited until the action became deeper and more regular and then attended to the fracture. It was a simple break and not out of alignment, so I split a pencil and used each half as a splint, then bound the limb with sellotape.

The following morning he was still dopey, but the support was in place and when I offered a few porridge oats, he nibbled a little. By evening he seemed much brighter and although I couldn't be over-confident about my treatment, I was pleased that at least he had survived the anaesthetic.

He was christened Herbie and although I wouldn't risk

the girls handling him, they became very fond of the little grey squirrel, treating him more as a pet than a patient; he, in turn, appeared to respond to their chatter.

I still used the gloves when I caught him, although he never attempted to bite again and when I finally removed the splints, he was so good I did so without needing to use a sedative.

After a further week the fracture had knitted well and the leg was strong again, so I decided, despite protests from the family, that I should set Herbie free. I was sure he would be able to cope with life in his natural environment again and I thought that this was the fairest thing to do, before he got out of touch.

It was a gloriously warm morning in late April when I drove him down to Fernhouse Wood in the cat basket. Parking the car in the small lay-by at the fringe of the trees, I carried him down the damp grassy ride to a spot beneath a large oak. Herbie danced about excitedly inside, as if he was fully aware that he was back 'home' and going to stay.

When I opened the basket I expected him to dart away, but he sat for a few minutes just sniffing the air.

'Go on,' I said. 'I'm sure you've got things to do.'

He hopped onto the corner of the basket, wobbled, then dropped into the long grass, took three extended leaps, then sat up perkily and looked around as if to satisfy himself he wasn't dreaming; he then took three leaps back to the basket. For a minute, I thought he was going to jump back into it, but after sniffing it cautiously, he took a further three extended leaps away in the other direction and sat up again.

He carried out this manoeuvre four times altogether, one from approximately each corner of the basket, and each time he returned to give it a fleeting sniff, as if he wasn't going to abandon his former security too readily.

I watched his antics for a long while as he ran hither and thither, each time returning to within a few feet of where I was standing. I tried to encourage him to run off by clapping my hands but he took no notice at all, so finally I picked up the basket and decided to walk away.

After a few yards I turned round and there he was behind me.

'You can't come with me,' I told him firmly. 'A cage is no place for a squirrel – now push off! Climb a tree or something!' and putting down the basket I clapped my hands once more.

This time it worked and Herbie shot up the great oak like lightning. Higher and higher he went, as if to demonstrate his fitness, until he was out of sight. Satisfied he had made the break, with a little tinge of sadness, I went back to the car.

It was turning into a warm balmy day and as I had no pressing calls, I decided to stay in the lay-by and complete some outstanding invoices I had with me.

I was there for some time and was on the final sheet when I heard the gun. The boom as the shot echoed through the wood startled me, for I had been deep in concentration over the paperwork and had forgotten just where I was.

Then I remembered.

In a flash I was out of the car, through the gap in the hedge and running frantically down the ride to where the keeper stood.

He looked startled, as well he might, with me bearing madly down upon him. The twelve-bore shotgun was through his arm, a spent cartridge at his feet nearby and in his left hand he held a grey, lifeless, furry body with blood dripping from its head.

I stared in disbelief.

'You bastard,' I said. 'You've shot my squirrel!'

I didn't shout, I just said it quietly.

The keeper, whom I know well now but did not then, was naturally mystified, yet instead of ridiculing my attitude, he said, equally quietly: 'Your squirrel?'

I nodded and held out my hand. He passed the little dead thing to me and I felt it, in the vain hope it wasn't Herbie – but as I ran my fingers over the right hind leg, I came across the small lump where the broken bone had healed, and I knew that it was.

44

I took him back home with me, although I did not tell the girls, and the following day I went back to Fernhouse Wood and buried him under the big oak.

I was never embarrassed by my action in front of the keeper, and when I met him later and fully explained, he just smiled in an understanding way and said:

'It takes all sorts . . .'

And, despite Herbie's tragic end, I did not give up shooting, at least, not straight away.

However, the following season, when I was invited to several guest days, the sport did not yield quite the same satisfaction and I found I was leaving more and more birds in the pretence that they were out of range, knowing full well that I could have dropped them at twice the distance.

Even my theory of only shooting for the pot was coming into question, for a brace or two of birds should be ample for anyone; bagging more was shooting for pleasure.

'And a vet who shoots for enjoyment is like an up-holsterer who slashes furniture for fun!' – those were the words of Oswald Brettner, a boozy old vet who had reprimanded me with that moral code when, at a point-to-point, a horse which I was about to put down with a suspected broken back got up, being only winded. I had remarked to old Brettner that I was relieved and that I would not have enjoyed shooting it. I never forgot what he said.

The whole uneasiness of my involvement with the sport was brought to a head after an evening of pigeon shooting.

In and around the Borders following the close of the game season, organized shoots to reduce the numbers of marauding birds took place most Saturday nights. Over the years I had found it a most exhilarating event.

It was essential to get into position early and I used to go to Wormcastle to join the Payne brothers. Just as the last golden rays of winter sun were being squeezed out over the Black Mountain, I would tuck myself in amongst the bushes on the edge of the larch wood.

Still and silent save for the murmur of the wind amongst the trees, I crouched until the first pigeon, the scout, came jinking nervously over the horizon. Cutting, weaving, dipping and feinting in cautious flight and suspecting nothing, it would finally land unharmed in the topmost branches with a noisy clatter of wings.

Then came the main flock; singly at first then pairs, then groups and then *en masse*. They flew in hurriedly as if, despite the apparent calm, they knew an enemy was about – and how right they were.

For then the guns rang out and the massacre began.

That Saturday I had had a good night by killing standards, taking home sixteen pigeons in two batches, tied by their necks with baler twine. Diana would remove the breast meat and casserole it in red wine to make a superb dish.

I had hung the bag in a small place we called the 'cold room', and was about to take a shower before settling down for the evening when the front doorbell rang.

In the porch stood a shabby little man in an oversize anorak, the light reflecting brightly on his balding head – and in his hands he held a pigeon.

'I'm sorry to trouble you,' he said, his body shaking nervously, 'but I've just injured this bird. Can you help me?'

It was a most odd situation, for there was I, still with bloodied hands from my sport and my sixteen victims hanging dead not many yards away.

'I was coming past Fernhouse Wood,' he continued falteringly, 'and it flew over the hedge right into my windscreen. I couldn't avoid it, it went straight into me.'

I led him round to the surgery and placed the bird under the examination light.

Looking at it closely, for the first time I realized that, pest though it may have been, it really was a beautiful creature. Its plumage was so perfectly formed and layered, the green, gold and violet lustre of its neck feathers brilliant in the rays of the lamp.

The little man was rambling on about how he had only

been going very slowly and he would not have had it happen for the world. But as he spoke I could see that the bird was dying; its claws clenched tightly one after the other, then they relaxed; its eyelids dropped gently – and it was dead.

The little man was terribly upset. I told him it was not his fault and there was nothing he could have done to avoid it. There were tears in his eyes and he even offered to pay, but I told him I did not charge for wild creatures.

I saw him to his car and said 'Goodnight' and then I went back to the surgery.

I felt sick.

I had not had the heart to tell him the bird had been shot. Poorly, of course, and it had managed probably to wing on desperately for a few miles until, exhausted, it fell near Fernhouse Wood onto a car.

Fernhouse Wood.

What a coincidence.

I have never shot since. Not that I mind anyone who does, but for me it was no longer compatible with my outlook. My point of view had been greatly influenced by an old vet, a man with a pigeon, and a little grey squirrel called Herbie.

4

Of all our family, the one I thought most unlikely to settle down was Tarquin.

I was well accustomed to clients, intending to move to another district, asking for advice on how to ensure their cats would not stray. There were quaint methods, such as buttering the paws in the hope that the amount of licking that ensued would not allow time for wandering off during the early days, or taking the cat on a lead whenever it went out for the first week. I generally advised releasing them for short periods prior to feeding, basing my theory on the fact that, when hungry, they would not stray far away.

Tarquin never gave any problems in this direction, for there was a wealth of interest for him within yards of the house, in the form of a grassy orchard where he could roam, sleep or hunt to his heart's content.

Sometimes, however, despite even the most stringent precautions, an independent 'mog' will defy all reasoning, such as the character I saw on my way back from Linden-church one winter.

The river had been bank-high for weeks due to the persistent rain in Wales and I was forced to make a detour because of the floods.

However, the extra miles were compensated by the scenery. The Wye, so lazy in its summer flow, swirled along in a broad, powerful thread; at Clifford it had breached the banks and, escaping from its well-worn trail, transformed the dormant fields and pastures into a silent, watery prairie. The thin wind rippled over the new-made lake, whilst skeins of duck, uncertain of their changing territory, squawked and chattered overhead. It was an enchanting sight and I pulled in to the side of the road.

As I stood by the car taking in the view, my attention was attracted to a thicket nearby.

A large cat suddenly appeared; jet black, save for one white ear and a white tip to its tail. Startled by my presence, it froze with a paw raised in a half step.

I was quite taken aback, for although one occasionally sees cats miles from anywhere, it was surprising to find such a grand specimen in that lonely spot, with the floods all around. Apart from the isolation, it is well known that as a species there is an aversion to water, and if the river continued to rise the itinerant member would soon be cut off.

It did not move, and for several minutes we eyed each other warily; then slowly and very cautiously, it lowered its paw.

I called such names as 'Tom' and 'Blackie' with little response; finally I took a step forward and, instead of retreating, it rubbed its head against a hazel stick and seemed to relax. Then, splashing noisily around the bend came the milk tanker and my furry acquaintance turned tail and vanished back into the thicket.

When the tanker had passed I called for quite some time, but the water was rising and reluctantly I was forced on my way, sad that I could do nothing to help the lone creature.

It was some weeks later when the Dukes came to the surgery, and there it was again, that very same cat – no mistaking the white ear and tip to its tail – but it was painfully thin and weak.

I told them I was certain I had seen it during the floods, but many miles away.

'He's a traveller all right,' said Mrs Duke. 'The previous owners of our cottage moved to Hay-on-Wye and took him with them, and about two months later he turned up at our place. We took him back, but he's done it again and must have been on his way when you saw him. I've rung the owners and they said that if we like, we can keep him – and that's what we're going to do.'

Apart from loss of weight and fatigue, the traveller had

survived well and with nursing would no doubt soon be back to normal.

'If I had only known his name, I think I might have picked him up and given him a lift,' I said, as the cat rubbed his head affectionately on the arm of my coat. 'What do you call him?'

'We're not too sure what his previous owners christened him,' she replied. 'But we've given him a new name: we call him Boomerang!'

There are countless stories of cats returning to their original homes, travelling fantastic distances over terrain with which it was impossible for them to have been previously familiar. How they do it remains essentially a mystery, and many are the theories postulated; but animal instincts, though often defying rational explanation, cannot be dismissed lightly.

It was such a peculiar 'sixth sense' that not only saved Tarquin's life, but brought him into my possession.

Goliath was a Charolais bull and a mighty fellow he was, too. The Charolais breed were becoming more evident in the county, despite a resistance by the Hereford cattle breeders. There were claims that, due to the exceptional size of the calves they produced, there were bound to be problems at birth; a suggestion that did indeed have some foundation with indiscriminate use of such massive sires on barely mature dairy heifers. There were also some difficulties encountered with the rearing of the calves soon after birth, for their rapid growth often gave them a low tolerance to disease and many succumbed in their infancy.

However Goliath's immediate problem lay in his feet. Due to his great weight of nearly one ton, and the hilly terrain where he lived, his hooves had become long in the toes, causing him to walk more on his heels than on the soles of his feet and upsetting his balance. He was in need of a pedicure.

There was no way one could lift up a leg for the performance; sedation and casting were necessary, a requirement not without its risks in a large bull – and Goliath was worth a lot of money.

One of my first jobs in Herefordshire had been to sedate a bull called Warrior, for an operation to remove his corns. That one gave me enough anxiety to last a lifetime, especially as its owner was not the easiest of men to please, and possessed of a violent manner if things went wrong.

Not that Phil Dixon was of such a nature, but I was still apprehensive about the job, even after several years in practice. Although drugs had improved in efficacy and safety during that time, the unpredictability of the patient's reaction had always to be borne in mind; for whereas in human medicine blood pressure readings, ECGs and other precautionary measurements could be made, in bulls, a lot had to be taken on trust.

The day came and I had decided to carry out the task in a large shed, which was vacant, the cattle having been turned out for the summer. Goliath had been brought in the previous day and deprived of food, a necessary precaution with cattle undergoing anaesthesia. Otherwise, a recently ingested meal could ferment and produce excess gas which the subject, due to its comatose state, would not 'belch' up. Gas thus unrelieved could cause pressure on the heart and lungs, with subsequent suffocation and death.

With all prepared, I injected the sedative into Goliath's massive rump, having to stretch to do so, such was his height.

Within five minutes he was feeling the effects and his eyelids started to droop.

'Now to get the ropes on,' I announced.

'Goin' to be a real tug-o-war,' said Arthur, one of Phil's stockmen.

'No problem,' I said. 'A few more minutes, and when the sedative deepens he will keel over by himself. The ropes are mainly to control his fall and to get him to lie over on his side.'

The system was known as 'Reuff's' method and was based on coiling a long wagon rope around the animal's

51

body, then looping it at the neck, over the shoulders and the flank, leaving a length over the rump on which one pulled.

This tightened the truss and where the rope entwined over the spine, put pressure on that point. This had the effect of paralysing the limbs which then buckled and the 'casting' was completed.

Arthur had prepared a bed of deep straw of considerable proportions for Goliath to collapse on to, and with the great beast now swaying from side to side we took up our positions at the end of the rope, ready to heave when he started to fall.

'Any minute now!' I called, as Phil Dixon, Arthur and Ted the tractor driver who had been kept back to assist, took up the strain.

Goliath started to snore, a sign his throat muscles were relaxing, then his knees bent.

'He's going – pull!' I shouted.

Hands tightened, muscles flexed and with much grunting and groaning the team dug their heels into the straw.

But Goliath sunk no further.

'PULL!' I yelled. 'HE'S GOT TO GO!'

''E's of a different persuasion,' wheezed Arthur from behind.

And indeed Goliath was, for despite our heaving and straining, pleading and shouting, he would not lie down in the straw.

'You'll need to give him some more,' said Phil. 'He ain't going like this.'

I was mystified. The dose I knew was correct according to the instructions, though I had to admit that the estimation of his weight might have been a little out. However, I gave him a further injection.

After giving the shot time to act, the effect became distinctly obvious; but although Goliath tottered like a drunk – he still would not drop.

'He can't stay up after all that,' I said. 'It's incredible!'

'Let's have one more pull,' said Phil, and we set to for the fifth time.

We were on the point of succeeding when Goliath let out a mighty roar that shook his whole mountainous frame and deafened the four of us. Then he suddenly seemed to shake off all the soporific effects of the drug and rose on his feet to his full height. His chest inflated and, throwing back his head, he surged off to the far end of the shed, dragging us like cork dolls behind him.

He was yards off the straw when he halted, though breathing like an express train.

With the steam squirting from his nostrils, he turned to look back at the straw, gave a soft, satisfied roar – then collapsed in a heap on the bare floor.

'What the 'ell got into him?' said Arthur. 'Is he all right?'

I was already at his head to check his reflexes, but they were positive and, apart from being asleep, he seemed fine.

'I just don't understand it,' I said. 'He has a dose and a half, becomes three parts doped, then produces the energy for a charge like that. Anyway, he's down now – let's get on with it.'

I walked across the straw to collect my knives and rasp and was on my way back when I noticed a piece of the bedding move, just about a yard ahead of my foot and at the very spot where we had tried in vain to lay out Goliath.

Then I heard a squeak and the straw parted to reveal the tiny, wide-eyed face of a kitten. Seeing me, it immediately turned about and attempted to burrow out of sight, but like the proverbial ostrich, it just buried its head, leaving its little gingery white backside and stumpy tail sticking up in full view.

I picked up the frightened little bundle and held it in my hands.

'There's your reason,' I said.

'You kind old soul,' said Phil, rubbing Goliath's flopping ears.

'Seen an' old cat dead on the road, t'other mornin',' said Arthur. ''S'pect it was 'is Mum. I know'd there was a litter round 'ere, somewheres.'

And that is how Tarquin came to our house, saved by a Gentle Giant.

* * *

Cats, of all animals, have adapted best to living in a human environment; indeed, it is said that they don't just adapt – they take over!

Tarquin was especially jealous of his new territory at Welbury and right from the beginning would sit on the wall by the gate, daring the opposition to enter. He was a most impressive sight, with full, flowing ginger coat and silky white ruff about his neck. His eyes were yellow, deep and mysterious, and his walk proud and confident.

Yet he was in no way a poseur and in my early days in practice contributed to the business in a very real fashion, for I had occasion to patch up several village cats who had come off worst in fights – only later to discover that their assailant was none other than Tarquin.

What a cat! He showed absolutely no fear and I often wondered if he was either remarkably brave or just thick. If not sitting upon the wall, at surgery times he would position himself right outside the door and clients would be very concerned that their dogs might attack him, little knowing that was exactly what the ginger devil was hoping for.

There was Kim, a pleasant enough German Shepherd whose owner, Mr Kelly, would exercise him by hurling a red rubber ball down the lane in front of our place, which his dog would boisterously pursue and triumphantly return with in his mouth.

One day, Mr Kelly's aim was not very true and the ball, hitting a large stone, bounced through the gates and up my driveway.

Kim bounced in after it – only to be confronted by Tarquin.

The startled beast stopped dead in his tracks. Then, thinking it was but a simple cat, walked up to the statuesque figure seated in the centre of his path and barked gruffly.

Tarquin remained immobile, save for the light breeze ruffling the guard hairs on his long coat. He raised no hackles, neither did he spit or arch his back; he just sat there and stared directly at the dog.

Kim, somewhat bewildered that his action had not put the presumptuous feline to flight, took a step closer and pushed his nose into Tarquin's face.

It was then, still without any demonstration of outright aggression, that Tarquin delivered what I can only describe as a right hook. With a looping action of his right foreleg, paw closed, he caught Kim with a solid clout. There was no scratch, no blood, no damage – it was just a warning.

It would have been understandable under any other circumstances for a German Shepherd to finish off such an arrogant cat with one snap of his jaws. But such was Tarquin's sense of presence that Kim blinked in amazement, and back-pedalled slowly down the drive and out into the lane to wait for his master to retrieve the plaything for him.

And never did he trespass on Tarquin's ground again.

The fact that Tarquin was of semi-feral stock may have accounted for his fearlessness and his development into such a beautiful creature, rather like a wild plant that has been cared for and cultivated.

I always felt he was a 'man's' cat and had a great rapport with him, leavened with a modicum of respect, for his degree of acceptance of others was, to say the least, very variable. Maybe it typified his insecure upbringing, for 'wildness and aggression' are often dominant factors in the less domesticated cat, making them difficult or even dangerous to handle. I learned this from Boggy, my very first cat who, rather like Tarquin, came to me by chance and taught me to respect animals and appreciate their natural instincts.

Tarquin was of the same mould and forever on his guard. Though he submitted to handling, he always exhibited a degree of tension and on being released, whilst not exactly running away, would quickly put a few yards between himself and his restrainer before shooting a haughty glance backwards; then he would settle down to clean himself as if all contact with human hands was slightly distasteful.

What do cats really think of us? It was something I often wondered as I watched him sitting there, staring intently at me in a faintly condescending manner, as I went about my business. The dimensional aspect of thought is something that one can only speculate upon in animals.

As far as sheep are concerned – or so my super-intelligent human colleagues tell me – one shepherd looks pretty much like your average sheepdog. They actually measured the response of 561 brain cells on Dales-bred sheep dangling in canvas hammocks in a darkened room, while showing them slides of faces. They discovered that there was the same brain response to both humans and sheepdogs – which is not all that flattering to us. But they responded far more actively to their own kind and to an even greater degree when shown other sheep with horns. Following this work the researchers suggested that animals recognize features rather than entire bodies, from which they deduce such basic matters as sex, social status and whether the other creature poses any threat.

Such responses should be instinctive, though with those findings in mind, I often wondered if in Tarquin's case he saw the world through the feline equivalent of rose-coloured spectacles.

It is accepted that whilst humans see in two dimensions, we are also blessed with the facility of a third, enabling us to reason in a way animals cannot.

Take motion, for an example: from a train the country-side goes flashing by, but we know it is actually stationary and it is we who are moving; to the animal mind, however, the element of motion is not reasoned and to it the exterior objects are the ones speeding by.

Similarly, understanding differences of quality, character and the intensity of objects is beyond the animal mentality, and although it sees 'a plant, car or man', it does not appreciate the differences between them. An animal's thinking is simple arithmetic whilst man's is algebraic, and for this reason it has been suggested that animals fill their brains with a fantastic collection of facts, leaving little space for intellectual development.

But whilst the results of such extensive deliberations by scientists may well apply to ordinary animals, anyone who has kept a cat will know that it is a load of nonsense. For a cat is no ordinary animal and as for not being able to reason, that supposition I can easily disprove.

Mr Bolt lived at the bottom of the lane that ran past Gatewood. The old gentleman, well into his eighties, had lost his wife some years before, but rather like Tarquin he was an independent old critter and shunned assistance of any sort. He continued to live alone in his black and white, half-timbered cottage, and although looking after himself reasonably well, due to his failing sight and waning energy he was forced to let his garden run wild.

It was a long strip of ground bordered by tall hawthorn hedges and set down to lawns and shrubs, with three flowerbeds at intervals along its length. During his wife's lifetime it had been cared for lovingly and kept in immaculate condition; but after years of neglect it had reverted to a wilderness that would have broken Mrs Bolt's heart – though maybe she would not have minded had she known what a paradise it was for Tarquin.

Due to his dominant character, it was not long before he had extended his territory and was found asserting his presence in the most unlikely and often prestigious areas.

He was discovered, on one occasion, fast asleep on the bed of the bridal suite in the Red Lion when the happy couple walked through the door; on another, on the back seat of a Rolls-Royce parked in the village; and once – praise the Lord – on the church altar!

Yet of all his special places, Mr Bolt's garden was his favourite. Amid a glorious confusion of shrubs and flowers, buddleia, honeysuckle and sweet-scented mock orange blossom, Tarq, curled into a ball, would snooze away the summer hours, pink nose twitching ecstatically from the sensation of the heady bouquet.

As a result I saw less and less of him, but to be frank, as

I was extremely busy with the practice, I did not miss him too much.

Then one day I happened to meet the old man as he was returning from the village.

'Tarquin down with you?' I asked.

'Tarquin!' he retorted rather sharply.

'My cat – he sleeps in your garden.'

'Don't know,' he said. 'Don't like cats.'

And with that, he stumped away.

The following day, by coincidence, a letter for old Mr Bolt was mistakenly delivered to our address; so that afternoon, I took a stroll down to his cottage to deliver it.

The iron gate hung wearily on its rusting hinges and squeaked alarmingly; but as Mr Bolt was deaf, its cry of anguish created no response.

I wandered around to the rear of the dwelling and knocked upon the kitchen door, to no avail. Knowing the old gent was bound to be somewhere about, I peered through a window. He was there all right, fast asleep in a chair, with a hairbrush clutched loosely in his hand – and on his lap lay Tarquin!

Never had I known that cat to rest easily upon anyone's knees, such was his suspicious nature, and as for allowing his coat to be brushed . . . ! Yet there he was: two of a kind, a cantankerous old man and an independent ginger cat, had formed a bond.

I slipped the letter under the door and left.

To say I was not just a trifle hurt by Tarquin's change of allegiance would be wrong. Even I, supposedly able to understand animal reactions in a rational manner, aware that they were officially regarded as lesser beings and that scientists had shown cats to be in no way capable of intelligent thought – even I still felt miffed by what had happened.

But as Diana reasoned in her ever sympathetic way, if Tarquin could comfort the failing Mr Bolt in his loneliness, our feelings were of lesser import. Of course she was right, and even when Bill Smart, the local handyman, told me he had fitted a cat-flap in the old gentleman's kitchen door, I did not mind and accepted that Tarquin had found another home.

I saw him occasionally when I went for a walk down the lane: he looked a picture of health and his coat shone luxuriantly. He would come up and rub against my legs and let me stroke him; but any move to pick him up was immediately resisted and he would retreat into the unkempt garden through one of the many gaps in the hawthorn hedge.

His leaving home, however, pleased one individual, and that was Branston, our Jack Russell.

He had come in payment of a longstanding debt and was so-called because he was a grandson of Pickles, a little bitch on which I had operated in very emotional circumstances, when we were living in Ledingford. He rarely associated with Tarquin and was really Diana's pal. For a JR he was possessed of a very amiable temperament and only on two occasions had he transgressed since our arrival in Welbury – once when he attempted to bury a bone in the village bowling green, and again when he escaped and took refuge in the bus shelter, refusing entry to anyone else, even though it was raining buckets at the time.

But although Branston was a companionable little chap, for me, he never possessed the same depth of character as Tarquin.

* * *

It was one afternoon towards the end of summer; I was in the surgery tackling the end-of-month accounts. Getting up to stretch my legs, I was standing in the middle of the room when my mind seemed to go blank – a feature which was not unique, for often I would find myself standing in that spot, having completely forgotten for the moment what I was intending to do. Di called it my 'absent-minded professor mood'.

Whatever the reason, it was quite odd that it should strike me at that precise moment, for my mental block was

59

suddenly broken by the faint sound of scratching on the surgery door. It was rather like morse code – three long ones, two short ones, then a gap.

Cautiously I turned the handle and looked outside: there was Tarquin, but in a state that nearly broke my heart. His beautiful coat was matted with dried blood, his eyes swollen and saliva dripped in strands from his gaping mouth. There seemed no life in his hindquarters as he attempted to drag himself closer to me; then he opened his mouth as if to call, but made no sound.

It was Boggy, my first cat, all over again. I had found him, caught in a rabbit snare, his back broken, and he had opened his mouth and mewed silently in just the same way.

But there was one outstanding difference: with Boggy, I had been a nine-year-old schoolboy; with Tarquin, I was a fully qualified vet. There had been nothing I could do to help Boggy, but now, whatever had happened to Tarquin I was in a far better position to help my pal and determined to save him.

'Come on, old chap,' I said. 'You're home now.'

Gently, I picked him up and laid him on the surgery table.

There was no snare, for which I was thankful, and from his condition I surmised he must have been involved in a road accident, for there were traces of oil as well as blood on his fur. Fortunately his back, though badly bruised, was intact. He was suffering from lacerations to the tongue and concussion – but the most serious damage of all was to his right hind leg. It was broken in two places.

I worked on him for many hours to counteract his shock and weakness; he was bruised internally and in considerable pain. Later that night, when he seemed easier and his breathing more controlled, I operated upon the broken limb and pinned the fractures.

It was a difficult task, for the bone had splintered and I had to search out the dispersed fragments before I could close the surgical incision. Periodically I gave intravenous injections of a blood expander, for I suspected there might be internal haemorrhage, but he maintained his colour well.

I sat with him until the early hours of the morning, when Diana awoke and carried on the vigil.

Together, we nursed Tarquin for a week. He refused to eat, so we fed him with a dropper.

Then Diana had a brilliant idea and one which I have used since on several occasions. She made beef-flavoured ice cubes and would gently rub his lips, cooling, moistening, and feeding at the same time. He responded well to this method, but still refused solids.

There was no doubt that, due to his facial damage, the sense of smell was impaired; this faculty is supremely important to cats and lack of it often makes them reluctant to accept food, so I decided to try him with the strongest smelling nutriment I could think of – some very, very ripe Camembert cheese.

To my great joy, he sniffed it, then raised his head towards me in a gesture of approval and slowly but surely ate the lot.

When the weather was right, we would sit him outside in the sun, turning him occasionally, for he was far from mobile; but gradually he became stronger and over the next few weeks regained his confidence, taking short excursions around the garden.

He eventually made a full recovery and then, despite all our care and attention, he went back to Mr Bolt.

Strangely, I did not mind at all, and it was because of something the old man had said. When I went to tell him of the accident, soon after it had happened, he started to cry.

'He's a wonderful comfort to me,' he said. 'An' I think the world of him – but he knew where to go when he was in trouble.'

His words made me feel very proud and happy, for I was sure that wherever Tarquin went on his travels and for all his independent attitude, he was still my cat.

5

Many are the reasons why bonds develop between man and animal, and there can have been none more diverse than those of Totty and George.

In both cases there was an element of self-preservation, though the motivation was worlds apart.

Totty had Alf, a Sulphur-crested Cockatoo whose presence one could never fail to be aware of, the minute the car stopped on the forecourt of the little country garage at the end of the village. It was a jumble of a place: two hand-cranked pumps, one constantly out of action; a workshop spilling over with a multitude of car parts, tools, tyres and leaking oil drums; a kiosk that sold tobacco, cigarettes and bottles of pop made up the business. As well as keeping the wheels of the village and surrounding farmsteads turning, it was also the local centre for chat, gossip and scandal.

There was, however, one other small construction partly hidden by the wooden kiosk: it was a commodious, netting-fronted pen which housed Alf. For this reason there was no indication of his presence other than his voice, which to the regulars was no surprise; but when a stranger alighted from his vehicle to be told, 'SWITCH OFF YOUR ENGINE, YOU SILLY BUGGER!' it was quite a shock.

Alf's vocabulary was wide and extremely choice, and many a genteel lady had driven off in a huff after a most improper suggestion involving upper cylinder lubricant and squirts of Redex!

The problem was that the manner in which Alf delivered his bawdy comments was exactly similar in both tone and dialect to his owner's voice; so the indignation of some passing customers was understandable when, after such a startling initial reception, the little man would poke his head out of the workshop and say, 'Can I help you?'

There was no doubt that Alf's attitude to the customers did nothing to promote the passing trade and Totty was fully aware of this factor; but as a bachelor, the companionship of his animals was paramount, his business coming very much in second place. As well as Alf and Tramp, the German Shepherd, there were several cats, some bantam hens and a few fantail pigeons; but of them all, the old cockatoo was his favourite.

Not that Totty needed to live alone, for he had several lady admirers; indeed, he was a most likeable personality and, with a good little business, quite a catch. Of the fair sex, the one of longest standing was a widow by name, Corah Butts, who had determinedly set her cap in some form at the happy little garage owner.

Her attentions were steadfast and no doubt she would have moved in with him shortly after they first met, but for one thing – Alf!

Corah detested the bird and the feeling was mutual.

Whether it was devilment or pure malice on Alf's part, it was difficult to ascertain, but whenever Corah was about he would embark upon the most lurid sections of his repertoire, screaming out blasphemies, insults and Anglo-Saxon words that would make a Devil's trident curl at the prongs.

'I'll not wed you, Ben Totty, while you persist in keeping that wicked creature!' Corah would rail, and Totty would nod in quiet understanding, though never giving the remotest indication that he would ever dispose of Alf.

In fact, it wasn't difficult to read between the lines, for despite not being man and wife, Corah still cooked, cleaned and provided all the home comforts without actually being in residence – an arrangement with which Totty was highly satisfied and in no hurry to disturb.

Then, one night I had an urgent call from the garage that Alf was unwell and Totty wanted to bring him to my surgery.

He duly arrived in his little van with his feathery companion tucked beneath his arm and looking decidedly limp.

Cockatoos, as with all the larger exotics, demand care in handling, for their beaks are like razor-sharp nutcrackers and can shorten one's fingers cleanly and in seconds – but Alf was beyond argument and lay on his side wheezing heavily.

Totty was very distressed.

'Fifteen years we've been together and never a cross word,' he said, just as if he were talking of a human partner.

I had to smile, for there were very few of Alf's words that could not be described as 'cross', yet I could well understand Totty's meaning.

'Old Tramp is supposed to be the guard dog,' he went on, 'though he's too dozy by half to be much use, but nobody can sneak about with Alf there. Uncanny how he knows a villain, and if he can't swear 'em off, he kicks up such a racket you can hear him in Ledingford.'

But poor old Alf was in no voice that night, and as I examined him, I had my doubts that he ever would be again.

Asthma, pneumonia, bronchitis were all possibilities, though I suspected they could well have been precipitated by some other factor.

'You haven't been giving him any mouldy food?' I asked, thinking of a fungal condition that localizes in the respiratory tract of birds, called aspergillosis.

'His food and water are always fresh,' said Totty, 'he plays merry hell if they aren't.'

'And his pen is dry and well ventilated?'

'Better than my workshop,' he replied. 'The window fell out right opposite and it blows a gale through there on times.'

My mind ran back to the building where Totty serviced the cars: they were always backed in with the rear ends next to the window area. If Totty had been revving up some of the old bangers he worked on from time to time, the exhaust fumes would pour out of the now vacant window and into Alf's pen and that could have triggered off the collapse. I suspected that Alf was suffering from delayed carbon monoxide poisoning.

I explained my theory to Totty and told him that the best treatment would be pure oxygen. If he had a cylinder back at the garage, a slow stream through an inverted funnel held over Alf's face could be beneficial. I gave the bird two small injections to help its breathing and told him to keep it warm and bring it back the following day.

But Totty didn't come back and I feared the worst; Alf had been a very sick bird and if my theory had been unfortunately correct – there was no real cure.

It was some time later that I pulled into the garage for a fill-up and, to my amazement and delight, was greeted by Alf's voice coming loud and clear from the pen, with all his usual colourful phrases and even a few new ones I hadn't heard before, which actually mentioned Corah by name!

Eagerly I went up the little alley-way alongside the workshop to the pen to take a look at him.

'I'll twist your tappets, Corah, you silly cow!' he was squawking. Rather unusually, he was not on his outside perch, but on the one in the enclosed, darker portion of his abode; yet he seemed to be sitting quite jauntily and his feathers appeared in excellent bloom.

Oddly enough, he paid no attention to my presence, just kept reeling out his chat, non-stop.

Yet the more I studied him, the more I began to wonder, for as well as not looking down at me, neither his head nor beak were moving, even though he was in full voice.

'I'll twist your tappets, you silly cow!' he was saying again. '. . . You silly cow, silly cow, silly cow, silly cow . . .'

There were twelve silly cows before Totty appeared, red-faced and flustered.

'Bloody thing is stuck again!' he said, diving into the pen, and within seconds the 'silly cows' ceased. 'You won't tell, will you?' said Totty. 'If Corah knows he's gone, I won't stand a chance.'

'But he's . . .'

'Stuffed!' said Totty. 'A man in Kington did it for me.'

'And you recorded him in anticipation?'

'No,' said Totty, with a grin. 'That's me. Nobody can tell and I always agreed with what he said, anyway.'

So Alf lived, albeit with new innards and a surrogate voice, enabling Totty to continue in a carefree, though slightly devious bachelorhood. Maybe, having managed so long on his own, he had become a trifle territorial and, like nature's so-called lower creatures, wished to preserve his patch and did not feel like sharing it.

★ ★ ★

My own immediate problem was also one of room to manoeuvre – that of the mini-surgery; late store-room; future clinical unit.

To be fair, it was quite adequate for the initial demand and was proving invaluable for the village 'small animal practice', which was developing to a degree I had never anticipated.

I had moved to Welbury mainly because of the available farm work in the area, yet already this new pet dimension was becoming obvious and I became aware that it was more than just the convenience of having a vet in the village. My availability counted for quite a bit of my popularity and I had no illusions that it was entirely my clinical expertise – something left in no doubt at all by a very attractive young lady with an equally attractive Labrador.

'We love coming to you, Mr Lasgarn,' she purred.

'I'm so pleased,' I replied smoothly.

'Yes,' she said. 'It's so easy to park the car!'

Yet professional ability and logistics apart, to my mind there was another reason why pets were more to the fore, and that was the very real need by people from all walks of life for companionship derived from a source other than that of mere human contact, a bond which, whilst transient, during its time gives as much or – in some opinions – even more than the so-called brotherhood of man.

There is copious talk of the balance of nature – biologists, natural scientists, long-headed philosophers, even clerics and politicians enter into the field of rationalization. Yet a vet, who meets people and pets on a down-to-earth basis, is uniquely privileged to see emotions at their most basic and our fellows at their most honest and sometimes most admirable.

If at that time I had had to say what fulfilment I had derived from my profession as a veterinary surgeon, I would have had to admit, strangely enough, that it was not entirely my technical knowledge of the diversity of animal anatomy, physiology, disease or behaviour but the peculiar insight into human nature, something one could not appreciate, no matter how many tutorials one attended or books one read. You needed to be there.

And if I had to give an example of what I meant – it would be of George.

He rang to ask if I would visit his ailing dog and quite firmly I explained that I did not visit 'small animals', due primarily to the fact that although my surgery premises were not extensive, I had all my drugs and instruments to hand and could provide a more comprehensive form of treatment if the pet was brought to me.

It was also a far more efficient use of time and cheaper to the client: vetting in the countryside had been thought of as relatively easy-going in the past when it came to business, vets not being the best of financial managers. Yet with the changing times, I was beginning to realize that the economics of practice could not be ignored.

'That is rather difficult,' he replied, 'for a couple of reasons. One of which is that my dog is not too keen on travelling.'

I had already quite a long surgery list that evening and, as it happened, there were several farm cases in the area where he lived. So explaining to him that it was the exception rather than the rule, I said I would call. He was very grateful, described exactly where his house was situated and I told him to expect me about mid-day.

The morning round went smoothly, with the Tuberculin Test I had arranged being so well organized by the stockman that it took half the time I had allowed. A lame pony, with a reputation for being a bit 'waspy', co-operated, and as the other calls were also straightforward, I arrived at Dinford House, the home of George Kinnersley, just on twelve o'clock.

The residence was large and stone built, with many windows and a long verandah skirting the south side, which faced the winding drive that ran to the road. It was partly shielded by three large beech trees, and though the lawns had been rough mown and the shrubs were somewhat overgrown, the garden was not unattractive.

Pulling into the access, just off the road, I got out to open the gate.

It was heavy and weighing down upon its hinges, so that I had to lift it in order to release the catch. After a struggle it gave and I was about to push it clear, when I heard a 'grunting' sound up ahead of me.

Raising my eyes to the corner of the house I caught sight of a small black pony. Thinking perhaps that was why the garden was in a slightly unkempt condition, I pushed the gate further open.

Then the pony grunted again, but this time it was deeper and continuous in tone – in fact, it was more like a growl.

I looked up for a second time and to my amazement saw that it wasn't a pony but a dog – a Great Dane, in fact – and it was hurtling hell for leather down the drive towards me.

I leaped back like snapped elastic and slammed the gate fast, just in time to create a welcome barrier between the monster and my body.

It was a frightening sight, for it slobbered and snarled, its yellow eyes flashing menacingly – had it been auditioning for a part in *The Hound of the Baskervilles*, it would have been a dead cert.

Fortunately the strong wooden gate was adequate protection from the powerful fangs, so there was no immediate threat to my safety. However, getting up to the house was another matter; the possibility that this monster was my patient, I banished from my mind, or at least attempted to do at the time.

Such a situation would create problems for the most resourceful, though as a veterinary surgeon trained in the handling of animals, I should theoretically have been at some advantage. It was extremely fortunate that I had a good understanding of animal behaviour and the confidence to know that the reaction of the Dane was perfectly normal, just an expression of territorial rights.

So, on due consideration of this vital facet of animal psychology, I decided that it was his property and he wasn't going to let me in!

Contrary to popular belief, like all vets, or those that I knew, I was not in possession of any superhuman power – the vocal techniques of Dr Doolittle or an insurance policy in the style of Androcles – and as the aggression after several minutes appeared to show no signs of abatement, I decided that a sensible move would be to pop to the phone kiosk down the road, ring the house and ask for assistance.

I was on the point of returning to the car when, as if a switch had been thrown, the Great Dane suddenly went quiet.

The transformation was astonishing. It backed off from the gate, gave a whimper and turned towards the house.

I watched it wander slowly up the drive and as I did so, my eye caught sight of a figure in the distance. It was George Kinnersley who raised an arm, beckoning me to enter. It was a restricted movement and I was then aware of the other reason he preferred a visit, rather than coming to the surgery, for George Kinnersley was paralysed and sitting in a wheelchair.

'Sorry about the reception,' he said, when I eventually arrived. 'Nero gets a bit excitable, but there's no real harm in him these days.'

'These days . . .?' I questioned.

'Reformed character now,' explained George. 'That is

how I came to have him – too savage, due for the chop. So I took him in.'

My perplexity must have been obvious. 'Surprised, eh?' he said. 'A lot of people are. Come on in and I'll tell you all about it.'

During this time, Nero had been standing behind me, and whilst I did not want to appear distrustful of his master's control, the revelation as to his previous character, coupled with his recent performance at the gate, made me wary.

In view of this I turned to keep the menace in my sights. He looked directly at me in a rather contemptuous manner, then, as if to endorse his sentiment, went across to my car, cocked his leg and nearly washed the vehicle away.

'Not much wrong with his waterworks,' I observed.

'No,' said George. 'That department is all right. It's his teeth I want you to look at.' With that, he propelled his chair towards the verandah. 'Come on,' he said, sensing my apprehension. 'He'll follow.'

And having no doubt that he would, with mixed feelings I went to the house.

George Kinnersley had been a big man: but though his shoulders were still broad, his arms sagged and his hands were frail and bent. A thick tartan blanket covered his waist and legs, the toes of carpet slippers peeping from beneath.

But his face was full-bearded and his eyes twinkled. They say the eyes are the mirror of the soul and, that being true, George Kinnersley, despite his affliction, appeared to be a merry fellow – an assumption I later discovered to be well founded.

His room was large and multipurpose – a 'survival room' rather than a 'living' one, with all the paraphernalia of disablement. There were hoists, pulleys, extendable tables and along one wall a large metal tube with hoses and a gauge.

'Respirator,' said George. 'I like to be as independent as possible, but sometimes I have to accept a little help.' He swung his chair round and motioned me to sit down. 'This packet took a fair bit of getting used to,' he said. 'I don't normally go into the details, but if you have got a few minutes I'd like to explain. It is relevant to the situation.'

'Of course,' I said. 'Please do.'

Nero had padded in behind us and when George appeared to have settled his position, went across and lay down by his chair.

'Good sky,' he said, gazing wistfully through the lattice windows across the lush valley to where shafts of sunlight were breaking through the fluffy cumulus, illuminating the patchy fields like theatre spotlights. 'Out of the cloud, back to the sun – that always got 'em. Pass over while they were dazzled; then before they could turn their heads, bank and dive. Right up their tail and . . . Whap!' He put his hand down to Nero, who obligingly raised his massive head to assist the contact. 'Battle of Britain days,' he said, shaking his head, a faint smile creeping over his face. 'Boy, did we have some scraps.'

I looked at the crumpled man in admiration; but for the likes of him I would never have been a country vet – perhaps never have been in being at all.

I was just seven when the war started, and my mind suddenly slipped back to Abergranog and Talfyn Thomas, the ARP warden, who came to school to lecture us on air raids and the Do's and Don't's in the event of such situations.

'At night, 'ew boys, at night if 'ew'm out an' 'ew hears Jerry overhead, don't look up! Don't look up, for 'ewer eyes do shine like cats' in the dark! And if 'e see 'ew . . .!' Then he would throw his arms in the air and shout, 'IT'S BOOM BOOM! GOODBYE DAIO!'

I never forgot it.

Now here I was, facing someone who at that very time had been prepared to fight for our freedom from oppression, even die or become seriously maimed to secure a future which the likes of myself and others took for granted. Risking his life whilst we boys were playing soldiers on the incline, slipping newts in cardboard gasmask boxes, sticking window tapes on girls' spectacles and filling inkwells with ARP sand.

71

'And that's where you . . . ?'

George smiled. 'Shot down three times, once in France and got back home. Then flew with Monty in the Western Desert and up through Italy; don't know how many times I swanned in on the old "wing and a prayer". Came through without a scratch – well, not anything that would count. War over, came back, went bathing in the Serpentine and caught bloody polio!'

For the first time he looked away from me and down to his lap; then he put out his hand again and rubbed Nero's head.

I suppose I could have said how sorry I was, but before there was any opportunity for such a pointless response, George looked up again and continued:

'I was on my back for nearly two years, in and out of that respirator, but I managed to get as far as this and started writing, fantasy mostly; it worked well as an escape and mentally I got to grips with things. The years went by, I sold several books and as a result was able eventually to leave London and come down to the country. Being cooped up in surburbia, I felt the open spaces would be more relaxing and refreshing; but the odd thing was, I found it frustrating.

'Suddenly to be able to see so far and so high every day and not be able to rush out into it, was devastating, a feeling I had never had in the brick jungle where I was living.

'It was then that my old flying instincts came back and I longed for those days again – crazy though it may seem – with all the risks and uncertainty that every waking minute brought. All those years when I had not given it a thought; yet it had lurked there in my mind all the time.

'The crushing thing was that this chair is no bigger than my old cockpit, and peculiarly similar in its confinement. When you're strapped in a Spit, it's pretty restrictive, I can tell you, and yet that sense of power, individual superiority, that unique freedom, was something wonderful.

'Just to have known it and died could well have been enough, compared with the bland existence of some folks;

to have known it and survived was something very special; but to have known it and be smashed down physically and mentally like I was, was unfair and suddenly it became too much.'

He sighed deeply, and as far as he was able clenched his fragile fists.

'My wife was happy here,' he said, 'but, angel that she is, offered to go back to London.

'Then one day old Mervyn who does a bit in the garden – and it is just a bit, too,' George chuckled to himself, 'but then he's not a bad old stick and will chat for hours, which suits me fine. He told me about another place he worked at where they had this Great Dane that had turned nasty. It was going to be destroyed because no one could handle it. Suddenly I saw a challenge and made enquiries to see whether I could have it.'

At that point Nero, as if knowing he was the subject under discussion, stood up and stretched.

I inadvertently reached out a hand towards him in a gesture of friendliness, but it was totally misguided. Whether he interpreted it as a threat towards his master I did not know, but he came forward, snarling evilly, and I quickly drew back. He stood in front of me for several moments, menacing and positively dangerous, yet George made no move to distract him. Then, of his own accord, he turned, sniffed the spot where he had been lying and settled down again.

There was no denying it, I was unnerved; my neck ran cold as a score of little pimples gathered under my collar. Yet it was not just the attitude of Nero that had contributed to it, though that was in itself enough; but that George seemed to make no attempt to intervene – in fact I even suspected he relished my predicament.

'Frightened?' he asked, in a manner that rather confirmed my suspicion.

'Yes,' I said. 'I know when the odds are against me.'

George smiled, but not with any devious pleasure.

'Forgive me,' he said. 'You see, I told them I wanted a guard dog. Well, with just the two of us here, my wife and me, if anyone wanted to break in and get awkward there wouldn't be much to stop them. I could swear – and that would be about all. So they came and said I could have him, but he was best chained or confined because of his unpredictable temperament.

'I wouldn't have that at any price and told them to leave him in this room alone with me.

'They took some persuading; but even if I am in this can on wheels, I can be a bit "bloody minded"; they said, on my own head be it – and so it was.'

My personal sensation of fear was subsiding rapidly as I became intensely interested in George's story.

'I shall never forget that hour,' he said, shaking his head slowly. 'No, sir. Short of actually attacking, that dog did everything else; but I'm not being pompous when I say that I never for one minute felt scared.

'You see', he explained, 'since I became disabled I've been closeted from any sort of realistic challenge. I've had the battle with myself as far as surviving, but that was internal; never, never since my flying days had I ever been subjected to such a powerful confrontation.

'For the first time for years I felt the surge of adrenalin; stuff I thought had drained from me for ever. For that hour I was alert, toned up, ready for action . . . alive!' He paused. 'How are you off for time?'

'Plenty,' I replied.

'He first stood and put on a big show of teeth,' went on George, now reliving the moment as all genuine authors do, 'his bark deafening me, but I just sat here and stared at him.

'Once or twice he lunged forward, but I didn't move; bloody well couldn't, though, could I?' He pulled enthusiastically at his beard. 'Then my unexpected challenge got fed up with that and started prowling around like a tiger, sniffing and nuzzling at everything in the room except me. I still had not said anything to him and gradually he calmed down and eventually came and stood just there.' George pointed to a curled sheepskin rug on the floor. 'I

74

was just about to say something when the bloody telephone rang and he went berserk.

'God! What a transformation! He dived forward and knocked me and the chair back into the corner. Then he charged around the room as if he was demented, ripping, tearing and bowling things over; he got hold of the covers on my bed and dragged them to the floor, pillows and all, and then he got hold of this.' George fished from beneath his blanket an old, tattered leather flying helmet.

'The only bit of sentiment I allow myself,' he said. 'Of course I had my gongs for the flying, but this was something very precious to me and I always sleep with it under my head.'

He rubbed the scarred leather gently between his fingers and for a split second was lost in memories of other days. Then he recovered:

'When he got hold of it and was about to tear it to pieces, I really lost my cool.

'"Put that down, you black bastard!" I yelled. "That's mine!" And do you know, he stopped ragging it and looked up at me with absolute amazement.

'"Now bring it here!" I ordered. And he did. And ever since then he's been my dog.'

I sat there thinking it was some tale; but it had to be believed for how else could a cripple in a wheelchair come to terms with such a creature?

But George was still in full flow.

'Some things are sent for a purpose,' he said, 'and this old flea-bag was one of them; ever since then, and that was three years ago, I've been alive again; because, you see, he is part of me – an extension of myself, both physically and mentally.

'When we go on our trips around the lanes, he goes where I would like to go: into the fields, amongst the trees, splashes in the ponds; small distances maybe – but in my state, a whole world.

'And he's powerful, tough, aggressive, fearsome – that dog would kill for me – and I am his master!' The last sentence was uttered with authority and firm belief, and who was I to grudge it? 'You understand?' he said. 'At this moment you are more disabled than me.'

It was an interesting thought and one which I found slightly amusing despite the circumstances.

'You're coming at my tail now, aren't you?' I said. 'Back to the sun, out of the clouds, turn, bank and . . . Whap!'

'Got it!' said George. 'Got it, Hugh Lasgarn!' He beamed delightedly.

'You are the first I've ever really explained this to, because you will be the only person probably ever to handle Nero, and that's why I had to tell you. Great!' he said. 'That's just great!'

Yes. Great it may well have been, but suddenly I remembered the real purpose of my visit and for me the euphoria of the moment paled into reality.

'Now what about his teeth?' I asked, in as steady a tone as I could muster.

'Yes,' said George. 'He's never had a vet near him for obvious reasons. But I have been concerned because although he finishes his food when he eats, he appears to have twinges of pain and occasionally will back off as if something hurts his jaw.'

'I shall have to give him a sedative,' I said.

George shook his head. 'I do not want to risk that, with all respect.'

'They are pretty safe,' I told him.

'I don't think he would like a needle,' said George.

It was sound reasoning, but unfortunately it would be the only safe way to dose him; giving tablets by mouth would be more unpredictable.

'How do you suggest we tackle it?' I enquired.

'I've got it all worked out. If you do what I tell you, he'll let you open his mouth, no bother,' said George, looking at me seriously. 'You can trust me.'

It was damned silly to try it. That dog could maul me beyond recognition and what use would that be?

'How did it happen?' I could hear the visitors around my hospital bed.

'Oh, he tried to open a savage Great Dane's mouth to look at his teeth.'

Nero was eating, and there certainly wasn't much wrong with his general health, so why risk it? Give him some tablets on the supposition that there could be an inflammation of his gums – that was it. Then if it did not improve, I would have time to think of something else.

I was about to explain this tactic when George said: 'Of course, if you don't fancy it, you can always walk away.'

Maybe that was unfair, maybe it wasn't, but the expression 'to walk away' coming from a man in a wheelchair struck home.

What had George said about his flying days, days when he had taken off across the bumpy apron in his little Spitfire? 'Risks and uncertainty in every waking minute'. All right, he had survived, but what wicked injustice had been served him afterwards. He was waiting for my decision, his eyes clear and steady as they must have been when they looked down his gunsight at the Dornier or Messerschmitt coming at him.

Crazy as it might be, I would have a go – sounds trite, but I owed it to him.

'I'll trust you,' I said. 'Now, how?'

George nodded with satisfied approval.

'Put your hands behind your back,' he said. 'That way he won't think you are going to be any threat to me.'

I glanced down to where Nero was lying; he was looking larger and blacker than before and his eye meaner.

'Stand up and come towards me,' said George. 'Slowly . . .'

I stood, hands behind me, within a foot of his chair.

'Now kneel!' said George.

What the hell was going on? I thought.

'Trust me,' said George. 'Kneel!'

So, kneel I did.

At this point Nero stood up. It was frightening, for he was now taller than me and I could feel his hot breath on my ear; at that moment I just began to wonder whether everything was for real. Was I going to be a sacrifice?

George had said his books were fantasies – this could well be his next work. The question was, would I be around to read it?

What followed was even more ritualistic.

'Right,' said George. 'Hold steady.' And with that, he put the leather flying helmet squarely on my head.

I remained like a statue as Nero edged forward and sniffed at it. He loped to both sides in turn, then to the back and licked my neck. Having approved of my head-gear, he returned to George's side, lay down and yawned sleepily.

'Good,' said George, in headmasterly fashion. 'Now go back to your seat.'

This I did.

'You can take your hands from behind your back now,' he added. 'Then, when you're ready, call him.'

I settled myself squarely in the chair. I could have done with a glass of water or, better still, something stronger at that point, so it was with a dry throat and a slightly croaky voice that I said: 'Come here, Nero. There's a good chap!'

At first he took no notice.

'Tap your helmet,' said George.

At that gesture, coupled with another call, he responded, opening just one eye, like a drowsy alligator.

On the third call he got up, padded over to my chair and stood with his head on my lap.

'Now open his mouth,' said George.

By now, mesmerized by the bizarre development of the whole situation, with left hand over his face and right underneath, I prized Nero's jaws apart with surprising ease and, though he backed off half a pace, he made no further protest.

His mouth was a veritable cavern, yet healthy and his teeth in perfect order; but on the right side between his last two upper molars was jammed a sharp piece of bone, the cause of his discomfort.

Without even thinking, I put my hand deep into Nero's mouth and, with the tip of my finger, flicked it loose.

The great hound gave a 'gulp', shook his head, and

obligingly deposited the fragment on the rug in front of me; then, with a relieved sigh, he laid his head back upon my lap.

George was mightily pleased and so was I.

'That calls for a drink,' he said. 'There's a bottle of brandy in the cupboard behind you.'

It was a welcome suggestion and, fetching it and some glasses, I poured out the drinks.

Glass in hand and thankfully sitting back in the chair, I tugged off the helmet.

'A . . . a . . . a . . . ah!' exclaimed George, just as Nero moved towards me. 'Leave it!'

Instantly, I cottoned on to the reason.

'Wilco and out!' I replied, with a snappy salute.

Then I sat there with the magic hat upon my head, supping a very fine Hennessy and feeling like a cross between Biggles and Androcles. Boyhood heroes, though they both were, I wondered how they would have coped.

Personally, I thought I had done rather well and drove home in quite a jubilant mood to tell Diana all about it. But just like a woman, she wasn't very impressed, and told me off for drinking in the middle of the day.

6

If the state of the sky had a singular significance for George, then coming to live deep in the countryside had also made me more aware of the elements and their changing moods.

In contrast to the comparatively urban surroundings of Ledingford, where wet streets and umbrellas indicated rain, and shirt sleeves and melting tar hot spells, in Welbury the weather was 'right outside the door'.

I had always been interested in forecasts and had brought a barometer back from one of my cattle trips to Finland, on the principle that any such instrument made near the Arctic Circle must be right for the job, considering the extreme conditions experienced at such latitude.

This I religiously tapped each morning, but despite its scientific advice, I always took note of the natural indicators as well.

Although weather patterns follow a seasonal trend, there are numerous signs that indicate daily changes. As well as my own observations, I also learned a considerable amount of country lore from my clients, much of it handed down over the ages, which made local weather forecasting an interesting feature of village life.

> Evening grey, mornin' red,
> Ewe an' lamb goes wet to bed

– and so did the vet who might have spent all day in the sodden sheep pens vaccinating them.

> Wind from the East,
> Churls man an' beast

– and any cows down with milk fever took much longer to get back on their feet. And one of my favourites:

> Frost in November to hold a duck,
> There follows a winter of slush and muck!

These old country sayings held a lot of truth.

Amongst my patients, too, there were weather forecasters. There was Sam, a springer spaniel who always developed a rash just before a spell of hot weather, a symptom that I decided was a result of flea infestation. My suggestion, however was hotly refuted by Sam's owner who maintained it was definitely a 'weather sign'.

Max was a thin black Tom, whose whiskers were reputed to become stiff before fine weather and droopy before wet.

Then there was Sidney, a large, white, odoriferous billy goat whose domain was a paddock at the back of Bay Tree Cottage on the far side of the village, who was more efficient at predicting the weather than any animal I ever knew. According to the Widow Briggs, whose goat he was, Sidney's movements up and down the banky pasture were an unfailing pointer to forthcoming meteorological changes. If he grazed high on the paddock and in full view of the village populace, then weather would be fine. Grazing with the wind was an indication of light showers, and the lower down the field he was seen, the poorer the weather, its degree further defined by his direction.

So the expression 'Sidney's got 'is arse to the wind', when heard in the village, meant it was going to rain; though many a visitor, hearing the saying without understanding its import, was not surprisingly baffled.

To those who think they know better, it all may have appeared a bit of country 'eyewash'; but many a local housewife, Diana included, would check on Sidney's location before putting out their washing.

So when Sidney fell ill, it was more than just the Widow Briggs who was concerned, for no washing was hung out for many days until his indisposition was discovered.

I had been summoned the day after he collapsed. Poor old Sidney, when I saw him, was just a shadow of his former self; for though he was much beloved by many for his forecasts, the sentiment was not reciprocated.

He was in truth a distinctly truculent individual and devious with it, having the habit of sidling up to strangers in a most amicable fashion, lulling them into a false sense of security before lowering his head and charging them off his territory with his formidable horns and the snort and pace of the Coronation Scot at full steam.

When I arrived at Bay Tree Cottage he was lying in the straw, shivering and shaking, his eyes glazed and his vastly distended stomach emitting cavernous rumblings; yet far from being distressed, his owner, the Widow Briggs was distinctly irate.

'He's only got himself to blame,' she stormed, 'the greedy goat! As if I didn't feed him enough!'

My puzzlement at the outburst registered, for she apologized forthwith and explained what had happened, though I had to read between the lines to get the true picture.

Apparently the Widow Briggs gave 'tea and buns' to a local farmer when he was in the village. Not that his presence was ever advertised, for he would park his pick-up truck in the shed at the back of the yard, rendering it quite invisible from the road. Two days previously, he had collected some bags of feed barley from the local corn merchant, and before returning home had stopped off for his 'refreshment'.

Sidney, on the morning in question, was on one of his 'walk-abouts', and took a particular interest in the parked vehicle. How he managed to unhitch the tailboard will always be a complete mystery, but then goats are quite unique in their talents and it would be futile to speculate; suffice it to say that he located the sacks and dug in. Frankly, he must have thought it was his birthday, for one prod of his horns and manna, or in fact barley, from heaven came raining down upon him. After gorging himself recklessly on the unexpected feast, he retired to his quarters for a post-prandial snooze.

The Widow Briggs' guest failed to notice the leaking

bags on departing and drove off, leaving a fine trail of damning evidence of his movements all the way home. No wonder the village was interested in Sidney!

The cause of the problem having been revealed, the diagnosis was straightforward – Sidney was suffering from a 'goat-size' hangover!

With such an intake of fresh barley, his stomach had acted like a vat, causing rapid fermentation. The bacterial content of his rumen produced not only alcohol, but an acidosis; and debilitating as the first product was, the second was far more serious and could in some cases prove fatal if not treated rapidly.

Large quantities of sodium bicarbonate by stomach tube were followed by equally large quantities of coffee. Thiamine, a B vitamin, was injected into his jugular vein to assist the digestion and liver function; and antibiotics to control unfriendly bacteria completed the treatment.

Happy to say, Sidney recovered and the washing was soon back on the line in Welbury, although I did hear tell that the farmer in question shaved off his beard, because every time he looked in the mirror it reminded him of 'that bloody goat'.

How animals respond to weather makes a fascinating study and, in particular, the behaviour of bees.

I learned bee-lore from the same Widow Briggs, who kept hives in her orchard. She was full of rhymes:

> A bee swarm in May, 'tis worth a load of hay,
> A bee swarm in June, 'tis worth a silver spoon,
> But a swarm in July, 'tain't worth a fly.

And if the bees were 'furious', then thunder was on the way.

I remembered hearing her mention they were in just such a state one morning when I stood behind her in the post office, where she took her honey for sale. And how right they had been, I thought, as I drove up the valley later on to visit Jim Peel at Rowan's Bank, a smallholding tucked away in the lower folds of the Black Mountain. A nervous breeze fingered the heads of the ripening corn, but the air was heavy despite it and the sky dull and leaden, more like a November day than midsummer.

As I opened the road gate, the first clap of thunder rumbled in the background. 'Coals down the cellar,' my mother would say, 'I expect your Aunt Min is wetting her knives.'

Aunt Min was full of superstitions and thought her action avoided her cutlery attracting lightning; she would also put an onion on her bed during a storm, for the same reason. I remember pulling her leg about it on one occasion, only to be smartly rebuked by her saying: 'You can laugh, but lightning has never struck this house yet!'

And come to think of it, it never did.

* * *

Jim Peel's was a mixed holding of some sixty acres and very similar in style to Brynheulog, a farm in the Usk valley where I had worked as a student. The walls of the low-slung, slate-roofed buildings were bright with whitewash despite the dullness of the day. All the gates hung well and swung easily, the dogs were friendly, the stock well cared for and the hospitality sincere. Jim Peel, though not a larger farmer, was complete in his husbandry; what he bred he finished, selling lambs, pigs and cattle fat from the farm, and nothing left Rowan's Bank that was not 'quality'.

He had asked me to call to see his two bacon pigs that had suddenly refused their food. Jim was in the yard when I pulled in and Mrs Peel, as always, came to the door of the farmhouse, waved and asked if I had 'time for a bite'.

'No change in feeding,' said Jim as we walked across to the pens. 'Water is good and no shortage, bedding clean and dry . . .'

'And never been sick nor sorry,' I added.

'Not till today,' he said. 'Happy as two spinning tops. I always reckon a happy pig is a healthy pig an' a good doer.'

With that I fully agreed, for pig farming, like so much of the livestock industry, was becoming increasingly intensive in the interests of economy.

Just a few miles away a new unit was already under construction, where I understood that sow-stalls were to be included; in these the animals would spend their lives, their movements restricted and their social contacts denied and I wondered, if ever I was asked to do the work there, how I would feel about it.

No doubt it would be a difficult system to accept and certainly one to which Jim Peel would never subscribe, yet consumer demand with government compliance for cheap food created a dilemma for both farmer and vet when aspects of animal welfare were taken into consideration.

In comparison, the two Large White baconers were in four-star accommodation of the old-fashioned sty type: warm, clean and with room to take the air outside if they so wished – but on the occasion of my visit, they did not wish.

They lay, side by side, breathing noisily and twitching sporadically; a symptom which seemed more indicative of irritation than nervous debility. I slapped their well-covered flanks, but the only response was a vexed grunt as they refused to budge. Their temperatures were 107° and 108° respectively, well above the accepted norm of 103°, yet though their breathing was laboured, when I applied my stethoscope there was no sign of pneumonia.

It was when I ran my hand over their bristly skin that the clues fell into place, for I could detect a series of small raised patches distributed over their bodies and on closer examination discovered them to be of a bluish tinge and diamond shape.

Jim's baconers were suffering from Swine Erysipelas.

The soil organism that causes the condition is common in its distribution and for some reason can lie dormant in the pig's body after gaining entry. A trigger factor is needed to spark off the symptoms and thundery weather is one of them – a reverse of the idea that animals can forecast weather conditions, for in the case of Erysipelas, the weather forecasts the animal's condition. Fortunately the response to penicillin injections given early in the course of the disease is excellent and I had no doubt that the baconers would soon be back on their feet and as happy as spinning tops once more.

Jim was relieved at my prognosis and together we went to the house. Inside, the table had been laid with cheese, pickle and cold beef, with homemade bread and fresh salad from the garden.

Mrs Peel had already prepared a bowl of hot water and as I washed up, through the small window in front of me I spied Will, Jim's son, coming across the yard.

I had first met Will at Granstone, where he was a groom to Lord Pendleford, when I was there attending to Napoleon, the aged Maltese stud dog belonging to his Lordship's sister. A message had come from Will to say that Lord Pendleford's favourite hunter, Kismet, had fallen ill, and I had gone to the stables to treat him.

I was drying my hands when he came through the door.

'What's wrong with our pigs, Mr Lasgarn?' Mrs Peel was asking.

'Diamond Disease,' I said. 'Hello, Will – how are things?'

He stopped in his tracks. For a fleeting moment I thought he was ill, for his face suddenly lost colour and he started to shake. His right hand went to the wall for support.

'Will!' said Mrs Peel, reaching out.

But he didn't seem to hear. He pushed himself up, gave a deep sigh, then turned slowly about and went back out into the yard, leaving the door half open.

Jim Peel crossed the kitchen and closed it quietly, then he turned and looked at me.

'Bloody diamonds seem to be haunting us lately,' he said.

'Diamonds?' I didn't follow.

'Have you not heard?' he asked.

'Heard what?'

'Will leaving Granstone.'

I shook my head.

'Tell me,' I said, sitting at the table. 'Why?'

Jim took out his pipe and fingered the bowl, then sat down opposite.

'They say he stole a stock pin from Lord Pendleford, a diamond stock pin. Used to be a man was innocent till he was proved guilty – in Will's case 'tis the other way round.' He put his pipe back into his jacket pocket, then with elbows on the table clasped his sinewy hands and went on: 'Lord Pendleford had a riding accident . . .'

I nodded, for that I had heard of. He had been hacking over the parkland, not on Kismet or it might never have happened, but on a younger, rather skittish mare. Something had startled her and unseated the old gent.

'He's over it now, though,' I said.

'Ay,' said Jim. 'Concussion and bruising. Will found him spark out and gave him first aid – loosed his buttons, undid his stock. Then he caught the mare and rode back for help. When all the fuss an' hullaballoo was over, they discovered His Lordship's diamond stock pin was missing – he never rides without it at his neck. Will said there was definitely no pin there when he came across him, an' though they searched and searched the whole park, they never found it and they accused Will of stealing it . . .'

'Who did?' I asked. 'Lord Pendleford . . .?'

'No, not him exactly, but that bastard Crabb an' one or two others. Even Her Ladyship told my wife at an Institute meeting in front of all them women that it was a bit of a mystery – as if she thought he was guilty as well. Then the insurance men came down from London and grilled him proper, good as said they knew he had it – and that was the last straw. He's a good lad, Mr Lasgarn, you know that, but he couldn't take no more, so he come home; been 'ere two weeks now.'

'Working?' I asked.

'S'posed to be,' said Jim, 'but half the time he's in a brown study, mooning about and doing nothing.'

'And I should say "Diamond Disease"! Jim, I am sorry, I wouldn't upset Will for the world. I'll go and have a chat with him.'

'Would you, Mr Lasgarn?' Mrs Peel was standing near, teapot in hand. 'He thinks a lot of you.'

The lad was leaning on the gate at the back of the rickyard, watching a spiral of black cloud drifting ominously down the valley.

'Looks as if we're in for a soak,' I said as Spry, their eager little collie, ran towards me.

He turned, his eye following the dog at first, then he looked up.

'Sorry about that, Mr Lasgarn,' he said.

'Bloody silly thing for me to say, Will. But truly, I didn't know.'

'Thought everybody did,' he said, with a wry smile. 'Biggest news round here since Ledingford won the Cup.'

'You shouldn't let it get to you like this, Will,' I consoled. 'Couldn't you have hung on just for the horses? Remember old Kismet at that point-to-point, the day I nearly shot him?'

Will's features relaxed slightly and he nodded.

'I thought 'e'd broke his back,' he said. 'Felt certain sure he was a gonner – then when he got up just winded, I cried.'

'I nearly did, too,' I said. 'I had the gun in my hand. Boy, it was close. I'll never forget that moment. Lord Pendleford understands, surely,' I went on.

Will nodded. 'Good as begged me to stay, but even though I ain't that brainy like some, Mr Lasgarn, I got my loyalties an' my pride . . . an' when them rumours an' bits of paper was goin' about, it was too much . . .'

'Bits of paper, Will?'

'Paper with "Diamonds are Forever" an' "Lucky Diamond" on 'em. I couldn't stomach it.'

'But, Will, you mustn't let it ruin your life.'

'Easy to say, Mr Lasgarn. An' I do try hard, but suspicion is a terrible thing, far worse than if you'd done it. You just don't know . . .'

'Surprisingly enough, Will, I do,' I said.

The storm was starting to break and the first fat globs of rain splattered on the cobbles.

'Let's go inside,' I suggested and together we sought shelter in the barn. As the lightning sparked and the thunder rolled, we sat on the hay bales and I told Will all about it.

* * *

Brack House was only visible when one got within a few hundred yards of it, for the flat, winding, black ash trail which meandered aimlessly from the road, took so many deviations that a blind cow would have got there in half the time, had it walked in a straight line.

Eventually the track lifted over a ridge and, in the depression beyond, stood the farmstead.

It was an impressive though slightly incongruous sight, for although the buildings were low slung and typical of the area, the house itself was four-storied and stood grandly to one side. Georgian in style, it had the appearance of a doll's house, narrow and upright, though the roof was in need of some attention and the walls, originally white, had yellowed, with patches of green-stained damp showing through.

There were twenty-one windows on the front, I know because I counted them.

There were four on the ground floor, five apiece on the next two storeys, four smaller ones on the next and three attic windows, most of which were broken. Of the rest, all but three were shuttered from the inside – two on the first floor where Abel Bartlin and his wife slept, and one on the third floor.

In that room lay Mrs Grayling, a frail old lady in her eighties. Bedridden and lonely, her only companion, apart from Sadie Morton who came in daily, was Smartie, a little tricolour King Charles, who was well past middle age himself.

I never enjoyed visiting Brack House, partly because it was a forbidding and inhospitable place and things never seemed to go smoothly. I had heard Bob Hacker, my partner, remark how some farms put a jinx on certain vets and, for me, The Brack was one of them.

The poor fortune in my medical achievements was compounded by the hostile attitude of the Bartlins. He wasn't too bad, especially if he had just returned from The Flag, a small pub that adjoined the perimeter of the ground. Abel Bartlin found many an excuse to get up there and folks said that the nearby fields were the best worked land for miles around – though it was mostly 'elbow work' in Abel's case. He was forever boasting about his market prowess and asking me in a cocky fashion to estimate the worth of a particular beast.

'What d'ye think I paid for 'er, Vet?' he would ask, plucking his braces over his fat beer belly.

I often priced them high, even though I knew he would not be asking me if they had been expensive.

'Paid through the nose you would 'ave, fer that, Vet!' he would chortle. 'Better not send you ter market!'

Calling me 'Vet' and never by name, was another disconcerting feature. Not that 'Vet' was in any way derogatory, at least when said in the normal manner; but there was an element of contempt when it was spoken at The Brack, especially by Gertrude Bartlin, old Mrs Grayling's daughter.

The first time I met her was on the winding black ash path.

I was on my way to the farm and came upon her in her large green Triumph, just as I topped the ridge to the buildings. We stopped, bumper to bumper, and she glared at me fiercely. Even through two windscreens and wet ones at that, the heat of her venom came across as her painted features contorted beneath her shiny crow-black hair.

She raised a jewelled hand and waved me back, but I shook my head, for there was no passing space other than near the main road, and the meadows, soddened by overnight rain, were far too sticky for me to turn.

For her it was but twenty yards back to the farmyard, but she wouldn't budge; yet when she finally passed me after I had reversed nearly a quarter of a mile, she did so without so much as a sideways glance.

How the unlikely match ever came about between her and Abel Bartlin I could not imagine – and a most repulsive couple they made.

The only thing that brightened up the place was the presence of Sadie who worked in the house; her husband was a mechanic and together they lived in the nearby hamlet of Penlas.

When Mrs Bartlin wasn't about and Abel was at the pub, after cleaning, preparing the meals and scrubbing the cold flagstones in the vast kitchen, Sadie would make a pot of tea and, when I had finished my jobs – aided by Sam the farmworker who was so old that the shortcomings of his lot were long past worrying about – I would pop along to the house for a chat.

It was during these breaks that I learned about Mrs Grayling and Smartie.

'Lord, she was a spanking woman when she was young,' said Sadie. 'Talk about work, inside and out – an' Mr Grayling, too, a lovely man. Only the Devil knows how they come to have a witch like that for a daughter.'

'How did she get to marry Abel?' I asked one day.

'It was the Trust from years back,' she explained. 'If the child was a girl, an' she didn' marry before she was thirty-five, the farm stayed in Trust.

'Anyway you can imagine, no man in his right mind this side of Christendom would take her on just for 'erself. But she was determined to get her 'ands on them acres, so six weeks before 'er thirty-fifth, she married Abel. How she got him nobody knows – some says it was one of them fixing agencies. Anyway me and Sam was the only witnesses at the Registry and since that day she's never mentioned it one way or the other.'

'And what about Mrs Grayling?'

'If it wasn't for me she'd be in a home long ago; they been itching to get rid of her. But she's got a right here, Mr Lasgarn, an' if she wants to stay, as long as I'm spared, I'll look after 'er.'

91

'Don't they bother, then?' I asked.

'Bother?' said Sadie. 'Left to them she'd starve to death. I do it all for her – wash her, do her hair, help her with her food, read to her, anything to ease the old dear's last days. Apart from me coming in each day and that little dog, she'd have nobody, nobody at all.'

In fact it was the little dog that brought me into contact with Mrs Grayling on one of my visits to The Brack, to attend to a cow with jaundice.

When I had finished the case, Sam said Sadie particularly wanted to see me, so after cleaning up my kit I went over to the house.

She was waiting for me in the kitchen with an anxious look on her face.

'It's Smartie, Mr Lasgarn. He's not at all well and Mrs Grayling is ever so upset,' she said, nearly in tears. 'I told that madam a couple of days ago and asked her to send for you, but she said it wasn't worth it as both of them were on their last legs anyway. But he's ever so sick, Mr Lasgarn, and now she's in town – would you have a look at him?'

The room was smaller than I would have imagined from the outside and dark, but despite the gloom the air was fresh and clean. The bed, a mighty brass knobbed affair, filled most of it, while against the wall stood a great mahogany wardrobe with a central mirror, eroded for the most part by damp. There was a dressing table and commode, an aspidistra on a stand, and upon the walls hung two ornately framed paintings of Highland cattle wandering through the mists.

Amidst this sombre collection of furniture lay the diminutive figure of Mrs Grayling, adorned in a white nightdress, and on the counterpane beside her rested the little King Charles.

'Mr Lasgarn, the vet,' said Sadie, quietly as she puffed up the pillows. 'He's come to look at Smartie.'

Mrs Grayling raised her head like a surprised child, but

from the grey-blue shadows in her eyes I knew she had cataracts and could not see me well.

Then she held out a scrawny hand and I took it. It was an odd sensation, for though she had poor vision there seemed to be a strong power of communication in her grasp, clawing yet positive, as if all her ebbing energy was concentrated in those thin, clinging fingers.

There was a local saying to describe old folk as being 'all skin and grief'; with little Mrs Grayling it was 'all sense and grip', and though her visual and even speech faculties were fading and many would say she was senile, with my experience, through her hands alone I could tell that she was very much aware of what was going on.

Maybe it was a veterinary surgeon's appreciation of vital reaction which differs from the assessment often made by medical practitioners; for vets, dealing with subjects that cannot communicate by human parameters, may well understand more readily the signals when humans lose their finer senses and are discarded by their fellows as being unable to mediate for themselves.

'You are a kind man,' she said. 'I can tell. And I know you will help Smartie. I wish I was an animal, then you could help me, too.' She gave a forced, whispery laugh, her eyes directed at the drab ceiling whilst her other hand, the one that wasn't clutching mine, gently ruffled the little dog's left ear. 'He's like me,' she said, 'running out of sap. My roots are shrivelled and it's time to fade away. But until I do, I would dearly love to have him with me – he's all I've got. My little one and Sadie . . . these two. They don't understand down there, can't see the back of me soon enough . . . But he's not well, I know he isn't, and I don't want him to suffer.'

'You are not shrivelling away,' I said, 'and neither is Smartie . . .'

'It's true, Mr Lasgarn,' she said, gripping my hand even more tightly. 'Old age is a curse. I'm in the way . . . and I don't care what anybody says . . . and the sooner I'm gone, the better. If it were not for Sadie and this little thing I'd go tonight, God knows I would, if He'd have me.'

While she had been talking I had been running my hand over the little dog; he seemed nervous and shivered at my attention. Overweight he certainly was, which was understandable considering his inactivity.

His breathing was distinctly laboured, even though he was at rest, and I decided to examine his chest.

'Just want to listen to his heart,' I said, gently detaching myself from her grasp, but as I did she clutched my arm with her other hand.

'You must excuse my chatter,' she said, 'but yours is the first new face I've seen for a long time.' Then she smiled and said, 'Well, voice I've heard, anyway.'

Though Smartie still shook with fright, I placed my stethoscope gently over his ribs. His little heart was beating furiously and regularly . . . but not clearly. The beats were muffled and instead of being sharp and distinct, 'fluffed' into each other.

It was a systolic murmur that I could hear, an indication that the valves were weak and not acting efficiently.

'How old is Smartie?' I asked.

'Ten,' she replied. 'I had him two months after Dan died.' Then she sat up much straighter and tensed. 'Is he very ill, Mr Lasgarn?'

'He's got a ten-year-old heart,' I said, 'and it's just beginning to feel the strain, but I'll give him a couple of injections and that should help. There's plenty of life left in him yet, as long as he doesn't overdo it.'

I made up the injections and, with Sadie holding him steady, gave the little dog the treatment.

'There, that didn't hurt you, did it?' said Mrs Grayling. Then she reached out and grabbed my hand a second time.

'You'll come and see him again,' she said. 'Please. I'll pay you. I've got plenty.'

I glanced across to Sadie. Her face was taut as she rubbed her hands nervously down her apron.

'Yes, Mrs Grayling.' I promised. I'll come again.'

She smiled and we left and went downstairs.

In the kitchen, having arrived back early from town and

reeking of sherry, Mrs Grayling's daughter, Gertrude Bartlin, confronted us.

'What is the meaning of this?' she shrilled. 'What were you doing up there?'

'I took Mr Lasgarn to see Smartie,' said Sadie, her voice quivering.

'You what!' screeched Gertrude.

'He has got a heart condition,' I said. 'He is a very sick little dog.'

'Old age!' she rasped. 'You make enough out of us on the farm without treating sick dogs!'

'Mrs Grayling said she would pay for it,' said Sadie.

Gertrude Bartlin rounded upon the girl and half raised her arm as if to strike out, but held back.

'She did, did she? And who put her up to that, might I ask?'

'Nobody!' I said sharply. 'It's your mother's dog and she thinks the world of it. Surely you've got nothing against her wanting to look after it?'

'How dare you!' she screamed. 'How dare you insinuate that I don't care!'

'I didn't,' I said calmly but holding firm. 'As for the cost, it's just the drugs, which are not much, and I was coming here anyway to see the cow.'

Gertrude Bartlin's attitude cooled slightly, though her fists were still clenched in subdued anger.

'Is it going to die?' she asked.

'Not if it responds to treatment. I shall know better on Monday.'

'Monday!'

'I am coming back to see the cow with jaundice. I will examine Smartie again.'

I looked her squarely in the face: she really was an objectionable woman. For several seconds she stared back at me, then pursed her lips and blew – it was all but a spit, but not quite.

Then she turned to Sadie. 'I want to see you later,' she hissed, and flounced out of the room.

'Phew!' Sadie flopped on to a chair. 'Pity the bitch had to come back so soon.'

'Will you be all right?' I asked.

She smiled. 'Don't worry about me, Mr Lasgarn. A couple more sherries and she'll calm down. But thanks for what you done, I appreciate it and I know the old lady did, too.'

'Does Abel have any say in things?'

She shook her head. 'As long as he can sup his beer and put his hand up some of them tarts at the pub, he don't give a cuss.'

As I drove down the winding path to the main road, I reflected on my visit to The Brack – talk about walking into trouble! Yet I far from realized at that stage what was ahead.

As if it was meant to be, during the following weeks there were a surprising number of visits to The Brack, all for various but quite authentic reasons connected with the farm stock: lame cows, difficult calvings, worms in the sheep and pneumonia in the calves.

And, happy to say, my results were good and I thought perhaps my luck at that hapless place was changing for the better.

Even Smartie had responded well and seemed full of life once more. He was no longer apprehensive when I called, and yapped and wagged his tail with delight. So much improved was he that I was able to give him a complete overhaul – nails, ears and even a tooth scale, which improved his appetite no end.

As for Mrs Grayling, she too seemed much brighter and was full of conversation when I called. I would stay for a little time, sitting on her bed and telling her about my work, the places I'd been to visit and the folks I'd met. Many of the families she knew and revelled in the memories.

Gertrude Bartlin showed complete indifference to my presence, but Sadie was always about to take me up the dark, creaking, oak-stepped stairway to see my patient and the old lady. She always stayed in the bedroom with us, until one day Mrs Grayling asked her to go downstairs because she wanted to have a 'private' chat with me.

She waited until she heard Sadie's footsteps fade away, then she reached out and took hold of my hand, squeezing it with surprising energy.

'Mr Lasgarn,' she said. 'I want you to do something for me. But I want your word of honour that you will tell nobody.'

I was apprehensive at her request, but nodded my agreement.

'I am an old woman,' she said, 'and not long for this world.'

'Rubbish,' I chided.

She dismissed my remark with a shake of her head. 'You remember when Smartie was first ill and you came to see him, and I said I would like us both to go together. Well, he is so much better now that I know he will be here after me.'

I was about to butt in again, but she shook my hand sharply like a child who wasn't paying attention. 'I want you to ensure that he is well looked after . . . but not in this house!' She pulled the little dog close to her with her other arm. 'Sadie will have him and I want you to see to his health. Will you promise me that?'

'Well, if it ever happens, and it won't be for a bit,' I replied, 'I'll see to it.'

'I knew you would,' she said, then releasing her grasp she fumbled beneath her pillow and drew out a brown paper parcel wrapped in a maze of string. 'I also want you to have this. It's money for Smartie's keep and medicines. When anything happens to me, you open it and use it for that and if any is left over when Smartie goes, you give it to Sadie.'

'Well certainly, Mrs Grayling . . . but I . . .'

'Mr Lasgarn.' Her voice was firm and even authoritarian. 'It's my money, my dog. I daren't give it to Sadie or they'll say she stole it, or something like that. But I trust you, Mr

Lasgarn, you are a professional man and they will understand it from you. Please, Mr Lasgarn, do that for me an' I can go happy.'

'Wouldn't you be better putting it in an account or doing it through a solicitor?' I queried.

'Pah!' she said. 'Do you think they would let me alter anything now?' She shook her head. 'Do it for me, will you?'

With that, she put the packet into my hands and, with some misgivings, I accepted it.

'I'm sure it would be better off in an account,' I said. 'You would get interest.'

'Leave it in the paper till you need it,' she said. 'As for interest, I've lost all mine – I'm tired and I don't want any more.'

So I took the packet back to the surgery in St Mark's Square and put it in the safe.

I paid just two more visits to The Brack while she was alive; but when she spoke to me, the old lady must have had a premonition as to her time, for three weeks later, she died. Sadie rang with the news and said she was going to look after Smartie, and it was then that I told her about the packet.

'Well, if it don't cover all the bills, I'll pay for 'im,' she said generously. 'Will you be coming to the funeral?'

'Yes, I'd like to,' I said, and she told me when it was.

After she had rung off, I sat for a few minutes reflecting on her kind offer to pay if the money ran out. That was so typical of her, for she didn't have much, and with her husband's back problem he was only earning half the time and I knew they often had difficulty in making ends meet. Anyway, there was money for Smartie and I took the packet from the safe and opened it.

There were sheets upon sheets of brown paper, but I eventually came to the wad of notes, it wasn't that large, but they were in new condition and compact – then I saw their denomination: they were fifties and in total came to a thousand pounds!

I was staggered.

Never at any time had I imagined such a sum . . . one hundred would have seemed excessive, but a thousand . . . Well, it was certainly enough to see Smartie through, and the rest . . . well Sadie could surely do with it and deserved every penny.

The funeral was held in the tiny parish church of Penlas: whitewashed walls, black pews and good singing. The flowers in the aisle and chancel, arranged by Sadie, were absolute joy, for it was spring and their colour and fragrance lifted all gloom and sadness from the proceedings. No withered roots any more for Mrs Grayling, I thought, as they wheeled her out to her last resting place, but a new life and a happier one.

It was a fairly small gathering and after the interment I made my way over to Abel and his wife to offer my condolences. It was something I felt obligated to do, but was in no way relishing.

Before I could get a single word out, Gertrude Bartlin staggered me by saying, 'I hear you were given money for that dog!'

'Yes,' I said, 'to pay for Smartie's keep and vet bills and the remainder for Sadie.'

'For Sadie?' she screamed.

'That is what Mrs Grayling asked me to do.'

'How much?'

'One thousand.'

Gertrude's face went a deep purple. 'A THOUSAND POUNDS FOR YOU AND THAT WOMAN?'

My neck went cold as the mourners, taken aback, gaped at the outburst.

'I didn't know it was that amount when she gave it to me,' I said weakly.

'Liar!' she ranted. 'Don't you tell me that! Putting pressure on an old woman! You'll be hearing from my solicitor about this . . . you . . . you . . . YOU VILLAIN!'

And she stormed off to the car, with Abel in tow.

'Oh, Mr Lasgarn. I'm sorry.' It was Sadie at my elbow. 'I

said I would look after Smartie and she said, "Don't expect me to pay his vet's bills", and I said there wouldn't be any need as you had been given money. But I didn't know I was to have any, honest.'

Suddenly I became aware of the intense interest in our conversation and, taking her arm, moved to one side.

'I didn't know how much it was, either,' I said. 'If I had thought it was a thousand, I would never have accepted it.'

'She shouldn't have called you a villain, Mr Lasgarn. That was wicked,' said Sadie.

As I drove back to Ledingford, never in my life had I felt so rotten. Apart from being involved in such an embarrassing public outburst, I had been accused of misappropriation and exerting undue pressure – when all I was trying to do was help a little old lady and her dog.

'Fools rush in . . .' I thought.

And I had been a big one.

Bob Hacker gave a low whistle, sat down at his desk and put his head in his hands, when I told him.

'Why didn't you let me know, Hugh?' he asked eventually.

'Well, it was old Mrs Grayling's wish that I told nobody.'

'You realize the Bartlins could make a lot of trouble over this, don't you? She's a nasty piece of work is Madam Gert. "Hell hath no fury like a woman scorned", and with her face she's had plenty of that. Silly thing to do, Hugh. Silly thing . . .'

He stood up and turned his gaze to the window, and for a while just seemed to be concentrating on the view of the garden beyond.

As I looked over his shoulder, I thought how little I had ever appreciated the garden before. Too busy ever to stop for a moment and look at the lawn, sprackled with daisy patches; the cherry tree that never fruited; the rose bed, the lilac . . . how catastrophes sharpen one's thoughts and develop an appreciation for the simple things in life. I promised myself that if ever I got through this one, I would be a different person – cautious, disciplined and observant.

Promises, promises. Would I ever learn?

'What would your father have done?' I asked him eventually.

'Probably said you were an idiot first and then told you not to worry second,' said Bob, turning around. 'But he would also have said that the threat of High Court action is not to be dismissed lightly and we have got the practice name to think of. Best thing you can do is to go and see Phil Boon.'

Phil Boon was the practice solicitor, Welsh and a rugby man who had once had a trial for Wales as a prop forward. 'Kept out by a better bloke, blast him!' he would say in his jovial manner. Yet big and beefy though he was, with hands like hams, he was perceptive and understanding – an ideal combination for a 'man of the law'.

I had first met him in the Hopman Arms, a pub I used to frequent along with McBean, Bob Hacker's partner, because I was still an assistant at that time, and later at the local rugby club; so I knew him quite well.

He listened intently to all I had to say, peering occasionally over the tops of his half-specs, to emphasize concern whenever I mentioned doubtful points.

When I had finished, he lowered his head and rounded his shoulders as if he was about to pack tight in a scrum and pushed his elbows against the frame of the desk.

Then he removed his specs and said:

'Huw bach, you have put 'ewer wellie in it, haven't 'ew!'

Then he placed his hands behind his head, shut his eyes and hummed: '"We were only playing leapfrog." Oh, come on, Huw, a thousand pounds is a lot of money!'

'You don't believe me either!' I exclaimed.

'I do! I do! But young man – old woman. Money in a packet. Have you anything in writing?'

'No! I don't! I never considered that necessary! But she said . . .'

'She,' Phil emphasized slowly, 'is not here.'

'So I'll give it back.'

'Admission of guilt,' said Phil.

'This is getting completely out of hand,' I said dejectedly.

'It isn't yet,' said Phil, 'but it could do.'

A remark that depressed me even more.

However, he advised me to await developments and in due course I got a letter from the Bartlins' solicitors accusing me of misappropriation and exerting undue pressure, just as Gertrude Bartlin had done at the funeral, and further saying that unless the money was returned to the estate, High Court action would follow.

That night I met McBean in the Hopman. He was the only one who cheered me up.

'Where there's a will, there's always relations,' he said. 'Now take me uncle Pat, who farmed in County Clare. He had three sons: Conal, Francis and Michael; and when the old man died, in his will he instructed that as a mark of respect, each of the boys should put the sum of ten pounds into his coffin with him.

'So there they were, the three of them, and first Conal goes up to the coffin and puts in ten pounds in notes; then Francis goes up and puts in his; then up goes Mick, writes a cheque for thirty pounds, puts it in, takes out the twenty in notes and says: "I wonder where the old man will cash that!"'

Mac was a gem, defusing any strained situation.

Phil said there was a case to answer if we took Queen's Counsel; Bob said it would be bad for the practice; McBean said 'send the bloody money back'; and Sadie said she was sorry for all the trouble she had caused.

* * *

'So I sent the money back, Will. Though I still felt I had let old Mrs Grayling down in not carrying out her wishes. And the irony of it all was that Smartie died two weeks later, which turned the whole thing into a sort of black farce, for it would have hardly mattered anyway. Sadie sadly lost out, but she said she didn't mind and I am sure

102

she meant it. But for me, the stigma of suspicion had shaken me rigid. Just like you.'

'You got over it, though,' he said.

'Of course. The feeling of depression got less as other things took precedence, but the hurt to my pride still lingered. You will find that it does; but the way I see it, it's all part of life's rich pattern, as they say, and you will come to terms with it in the long run. Believe it or not, it will make you far more understanding of other people's problems, and a better man.'

Will did not speak for some time, and though the eye of the storm had passed, the rain still battered noisily upon the roof.

Then he stood up and held out his hand.

'Thank you for that, Mr Lasgarn. I feel better now,' he said. 'I thought I was the only one.'

'Only one, Will,' I said. 'Truth to tell, there's a hell of a lot of us about.'

He smiled. 'Mother has got some food ready, for the first time for ages, I feel hungry.'

'Well, if I can get you back on your grub as well as the baconers,' I said, 'it will have been a worthwhile visit.'

And together we made a dash for the house.

7

It was entirely coincidental that, when I arrived home, Diana informed me that Lord Pendleford's sister, Lady Octavia Grimes, had been trying to get in touch with me.

'It's a "parsonal metter",' said Diana, giving a perfect rendering of Lady Octavia's high-pitched chortle. 'Could you ring her "beck"?'

'Wonder if it's to do with Will,' I said, and told Di briefly about my visit to Rowan's Bank.

'Well, you never really got over it,' she said. 'I hope he does, he is so young.'

'Better see what the old girl wants,' I said and dialled through to Granstone.

Mrs Gibbons, the housekeeper, answered abruptly, as was her manner – then I could hear her footsteps clattering away down the corridor in search of Her Ladyship.

I had first come into contact with Lady Octavia at the Ledingford Agricultural Show, held in the grounds of the Granstone estate. Since then, I had ministered to her pack of Maltese with some success and found that, despite her often overwhelming attitude, she had quite an engaging personality. I enjoyed meeting her.

Mrs Gibbons returned to the telephone and there followed some confusion with the extension, which apparently only operated when the first receiver was replaced; then there ensued a period of 'Halloo-ing' from Her Ladyship that would have rivalled the good John Peel in the 'mo-orning'.

Eventually we joined in conversation.

'Mr Lasgarn,' she said. 'We have had a spot of bother and I want to enlist your help.'

Certainly, I thought, anything for Will.

'I would be only too pleased, Your Ladyship,' I replied.

'Good man!' she hooted. 'Knew you would!'

I was on the phone for some considerable time and when finally she finished, I went back to the kitchen.

'What's the matter?' asked Di, 'Hugh, you look awful! Was it about Will?'

I shook my head.

'The Maltese, has something gone wrong?'

'No,' I replied, sitting down at the table.

'Hugh! Tell me! What's happened?' Di asked anxiously.

'I have promised to give a talk to the Granstone Women's Institute on Wednesday night – their speaker has "corled orf".'

'Oh, darling!' she said. 'I thought it was something terrible!'

'It is, Di,' I said. 'It is. I've never done anything like that before.'

'You can do it, easy as falling off a log.'

Which was loving encouragement from Di, except that I had never done anything like that, either. The most public speech I had made previously had been as a member of the Pontypool and District Young Farmers' Club, an organization which I had cause to be very grateful, for though not directly connected with farming stock, through the YFC I was actually able to become involved in agriculture in my early youth.

I say not directly of farming stock, because it was my grandfather on my mother's side who was the farmer. He ran a small farm at Varteg on the windswept slopes of the Coity Mountain, at the top of the Abergranog valley.

An industrious man, so they tell, and an experienced sheep farmer, running his indomitable little Welsh ewes over the rocky terrain. Yet he was a man with an eye to the future and, though still in his early thirties, had taken an option on a grazing farm of nearly two hundred acres near Monmouth.

Sadly, tragedy struck in a most bizarre fashion before he was able to achieve his ambition: one of his best cows was due to calve and, with the birth being imminent, he kept an all-night vigil.

In the small hours, with much assistance from my grandfather, a fine bull calf was born. Exhausted but well satisfied with such a grand young beast to add to his stock for his new farm, he went into the kitchen and fell asleep in the chair – and during his slumber, his false teeth slipped into his throat and choked him.

But for that, my life story might have been a very different one.

However, the YFC made up for a lot of my inexperience in country matters and was an invaluable input into my future career. As well as learning to milk cows, lay hedges, judge livestock, dress chickens and become proficient at numerous other country tasks, there was Public Speaking.

In this art we were trained at regular classes by various local exponents, to 'stand up, speak up and shut up'.

Apart from aiming to improve our personal ability to communicate, the object was to provide a team to enter the County Championships held annually.

As with many things in those days – or so they appear now – the format was relatively straightforward; unlike the more advanced pattern of today, with Brains Trusts and Debates.

In the early days the team consisted of a Chairman, who opened the meeting with the 'glad to see so many of you here tonight having left your warm firesides, etc.'; the Speaker, who was the main member and talked for eight minutes; and the Proposer of the Vote of Thanks.

I had risen to the giddy heights of being first reserve to the Proposer of the Vote of Thanks.

On the night of the competition, minutes before our team was due to go on, the Proposer of the Vote of Thanks 'corled orf', as her Ladyship would say, thrusting me into the limelight at Cwmcastel Village Hall.

I was about to mount the stage when the Club leader put his hand on my shoulder and wished me good luck:

'Do it well, Hugh, and I'll put you in the Milking Competition on Saturday,' he said.

I was thrilled. My expertise was not very great, but I regarded milking as one of the 'real' jobs in farming, and to be able to say one could milk a cow oddly enough put one on a very high plane of respect at school. The chance that I might be chosen for that team as well filled my heart with pride.

I sat on the platform beaming like a little sun, as the Chairman went through his introductions and the Speaker did her stuff. In my mind I ran through the words which I had rehearsed hundreds of times:

'It gives me great pleasure to propose the vote of thanks to our Speaker this evening. I found her talk on – whatever it was – most interesting, as I am sure you all did here tonight. Please show your appreciation in the usual manner.' All very formal, all very old-fashioned, but that is what I had been told to say.

I was determined to say it well, for though Club prestige hinged on winning, there was a place in the Milking Competition at stake and I wanted that badly.

The Speaker, though she was still within her time, seemed to be droning on for ages: her subject, one of five known titles drawn from a hat previously, was 'Welsh Songs and Ditties'.

Finally she concluded and the Chairman grandly introduced me. In a loud and confident tone I started on my piece – but whether it was subconscious nervousness or the fact that the Milking Competition was uppermost in my mind, I do not know, but my vote of thanks brought the house down when I congratulated the Speaker for her most interesting talk on 'WELSH DONGS AND TITTIES!'

Well, there was no way I could talk of 'dongs and titties' to the Granstone WI, and for the next few days my mind was fully preoccupied with my forthcoming oration.

* * *

Granstone WI met on the first Wednesday in the month at the schoolhouse, a quaint rustic building with lattice windows, a high-pitched roof, and the headmaster's house adjoining.

Despite my hopes for an acute bout of influenza or a sudden call to take Hereford cattle to China, the day dawned.

Ivor Witts gave me curious glances as I rehearsed silently whilst testing his cattle that morning, and once or twice asked if I was all right. I dared not tell him what I was doing, for he was quite the local wag and I didn't want to be sent up at that stage. The odd thing was, however, that when we finished he remarked he had never known the cattle be so quiet.

'Just like they been 'ipnotized,' he remarked.

An effect that I hoped would also occur later in the day on some other females.

Bob Hacker had gleefully offered to cover the night calls when he heard, 'so that I could give of my best to the dear ladies of Granstone'.

Thus, at seven-twenty in the evening, after several glasses of water and trips to the loo, I set off. Diana having kissed me goodbye as if I was going to war, and driving as slowly as I was able, I arrived, sweaty palms and all, in the playground of Granstone school, right on seven-thirty.

The latch on the schoolhouse door was of the old-fashioned type that 'clacked' when pressed, and when I pushed the door gently ajar, it squeaked alarmingly, as I suppose I might have expected.

A musty combination of chalk, books and dead flowers teased my nostrils nostalgically as I stepped inside.

The squeak petered away, leaving an absolute silence.

I took a step deeper into the room, and through the gloom my eyes met the weirdest of sights.

At the desks sat women: women young, women old, women very old. They all seemed to be wearing glasses and their hair had been freshly arranged; and when I entered they all turned their eyes towards me – but made no sound.

All of them were mute, including Lady Octavia who sat on a high stool at the high desk at the head of the class.

I stood for a few seconds, transfixed by the scene. It was as if the class of years ago had suddenly aged and returned to their former surroundings which, unlike their mortal frames, had seemingly not aged at all.

Then Lady Octavia gave a loud, instructive cough and a bent little woman in one of the back desks gasped, made the sign of the cross on her chest, shuffled out of her seat and advanced towards me.

'Good evening, sir,' she said, almost curtseying. 'I'm Dolly Pump the Greeter.' It sounded most odd, but I smiled and held out my hand.

She refused my gesture, leaving me feeling a little exposed, and led off down the class to Lady Octavia, where she did perform a full curtsey and said in a voice like a nervous wren:

'Our Speaker, Mr . . .'

'Lasgarn, Hugh,' I volunteered.

'Our speaker, Mr Lasgarnew,' she stuttered, and I smiled, for it was not the first time I had been credited with that most interesting of surnames.

My first ever client, a dear old lady called Mrs Jarvis and her evil cat Samson, who 'normally is quite good, but when he wants to, can be a real bugger', as she so sweetly put it, also called me 'Mr Lasgarnew' and did so until the time she died. In fact, when I sent flowers, I put that very name upon them and there was much speculation locally as to the identity of the 'foreign' gentleman who had sent the tribute.

Having accomplished her most responsible task of greeting the speaker and guiding him safely to the high altar, Dolly Pump dissolved into a jelly and wobbled back to her desk.

Then it was Lady Octavia's turn.

She stood up and projected her ample bosom, rather like the figurehead of an old galleon which, in fact, she could well have impersonated in its entirety. As she rose, her arms came up alongside her, soaring aloft like the Statue of Liberty, and, cogniscent of the signal, all the members of the Granstone WI got to their feet in unison.

Then Her Ladyship, without so much as the bat of an eyelid, said:

'Miss Pringle!'

Over in the darkest corner of the schoolroom I perceived a piano and, seated at it, rubbing her hands in nervous apprehension, was the purveyor of musical accompaniment.

At the command she raised her arms above her head; and at the 'green for go' nod from Her Ladyship, swooped upon the keys like a hawk to a rabbit – and they all broke into song.

'Jerusalem' it was. I recognized it eventually and was unsure whether to join in or not – but only knowing the main bits, I decided to refrain and stood looking on appreciatively.

How thoughtful it was, I contemplated as they chorused away, to select such a greeting; being a vet from the valleys I considered it very apt.

I was not aware at that point that they sang it at every meeting and that it was, in fact, their signature tune.

Then came the 'business'; during which time I sat on the right hand of Her Ladyship.

It was during a protracted discussion as to whether they should take sandwiches on their forthcoming visit to Stratford-upon-Avon or whether they should have a meal at a restaurant, that I discovered I had forgotten my notes.

And while the arguments ranged back and forth – having a meal would allow them access to a toilet, whereas eating out would give them all syphilis (I think the contributor had salmonella in mind) – I went into a mild, but hopefully unobserved panic. Like the proverbial duck, calm above but paddling like hell underneath.

My mind went blank. I couldn't even remember my opening lines, leave alone the bulk of what I had intended to say.

I tried to think of Ivor Witts' cows and how I had "ipnotized' them, but nothing came. How I wished I was just having to propose the vote of thanks, as I had done years ago in Cwmcastel Village Hall.

In desperation I gazed about the classroom for inspiration, and as I looked at the desks and the bottom-aching

110

seats, the paintings on the wall, the dead flowers in the jars, I remembered that I had another experience of public speaking: back in Miss Webb's class – Class Two – in Abergranog Council School.

I'll do that bit again, I thought – straight, as I told it before.

In due course the 'business' was concluded and Lady Octavia introduced me with a grand flourish; but all I could hear were the words of Miss Webb saying, 'Come up to the front, Hugh, and tell us all about it.' And as I stood there, the faces before me faded into my schoolpals of yesteryear as I told the ladies how I came to be a vet.

*　*　*

One of the few redeeming features of Abergranog, where I was born, was that it was on the fringe of the Welsh coalfield; to the south-west lay the mountains and the 'dark satanic mills', but to the east 'England's green and pleasant land', just as they had sung.

In our valley, the black tips and turning wheels of the mine workings gave way to patches of woodland, small fields and farmsteads; one such oasis was at the back of our house and was known as Little Pant.

The owners were the Misses Prowle, two sisters, maiden ladies who were very proper, but regarded locally as 'a bit tetchy'.

Yet despite their eagle eyes, always on the look-out for trespassers, I was drawn to the fields, partly by the sense of adventure, partly by the fact that it was illegal and partly because it was so relaxing, once I had found the safety and shelter of the lower woodland.

It was sheer escapism, even in such a small area; the pastures were of the old-fashioned permanent type – uneven, lush, tussocky grass with scattered coltsfoot and buttercup and odd patches of thistles, whose spread was somewhat half-heartedly controlled by Arty Parry and his weary scythe. Arty was the cowman for the Misses Prowle and also delivered the milk.

111

On the odd occasion when Mother wanted extra milk, I would be sent with a large white jug to collect it; even then I was not allowed to go through the field, instead having to walk nearly a quarter of a mile by way of Bowen's Pitch and down the farm drive.

Arty's cowshed, with his five fat and happy cows, was a world unto itself; the animal-warm milky aroma, the crunching and munching of sweet hay, the soft swishing sound as strong hands powered the streams of milk into the frothy pail.

I would stand just inside the door and savour the atmosphere; then Arty would drag away his little stool and bring the milk to the churn, where he strained it through muslin. My jug held a pint and a half, which was three of Arty's measures plus a drop for the cat.

I would pay the money and set off for home with but a single thought in my mind: a swig of milk.

To hold the jug to one's face and breathe in the rich, heady aroma of the new-warm nectar was ecstasy, but to drink it was divine – how modern-day hygienists would shudder; but at that time austerity prevailed due to the War, and my 'swig' on the way back from Little Pant is still one of the most abiding and pleasurable memories of my youth.

Certainly things were scarce – ration books, sweet coupons and utility merchandise being the accepted norm; yet despite it all we had enough, and when real luxuries did come around they were all the more appreciated. That is why, even today, roast chicken, chocolate biscuits and bananas are still rather 'special' to me.

Yet, in a way, it was one of the side effects of the conflict that exerted a major influence upon my future way of life, that of 'Air Raid Dispersal'.

In the event of an air raid during school time, all children living within half a mile would be allowed home. Those living beyond the safe distance would have to go to a friend's house within the limit.

Because I lived over a mile by road, I was allocated a place in Wendel Weekes' house. His father was a bus driver

112

with Western Welsh and bred wire-haired fox terriers. Wendel was a good friend of mine and it was a good house to go to . . . though I would have preferred to go home.

It was Miss Webb, our teacher, who gave me the idea when she was telling us about maps, and how black lines were for the rivers, stripes for railways, brown for high ground and green for low.

'"As the crow flies"' she announced in her sing-song voice, 'means that if a crow was to fly, say, from school to Abergranog Park, it wouldn't go around the road, it would go straight from here over the farm and into the park. Much quicker it would be, wouldn't it?'

I lived on Bowen's Pitch and was on to it like a shot. If a crow could do it, so could I if I went through Little Pant; much quicker it would certainly be and hopefully within the distance limit.

I pleaded passionately with Miss Webb, explaining how, if the Germans came and I was separated from my mother, she'd be up to see the Headmaster in no time and cause an awful row.

Miss Webb took note of my suggestion and said she would have a word with Mr Talfyn Thomas, the Chief Warden of Abergranog, who in turn had a word with the Misses Prowle, and because he was 'chapel' and so were they, to my immense delight it was approved, subject to Miss Webb coming with me on a trial run.

It was a wonderful feeling to have Miss Webb all to myself and I remember it as if it were yesterday.

The day she came it had been raining and she walked with high stilty steps to try and keep her shoes dry.

The cows were in the second field, and when we started across I felt her hand grip mine so tightly that my fingers stuck together.

'You're not afraid of the cows, Hugh?' she asked, her voice unusually shrill.

'No, Miss Webb,' I replied manfully. And neither I was for I knew them well and on my illegal sorties had been through the field many times when they were about. And often when I was waiting for the milk I would walk up to them in the shed and stroke their warm, heaving flanks.

But Miss Webb was nervous, I could tell, for she quickened her step, forgetting the wet grass as we skirted the grazing bunch.

'Have they got names?' she asked, breathing rather quickly.

'Yes, Miss Webb. And I know them all.' Not only to have Miss Webb's sole attention, but to be able to teach her all about the cows was making me feel rather special.

'The big grey is Old Blod and the little grey is Young Blod,' I explained. 'Because she is her daughter. The red cow looking at us is called Lewis, because she came from Mr Lewis, Ty-Canol. The little brown one is very special because she is pedigree. Her name is Cystrema Golden Platter, but they call her Cis.'

'And the big black one?' she asked nervously.

I savoured the moment. It had had to come and I wondered whether she would react as the Misses Prowle had done when one day Mother proudly asked me to name the cows.

'The black one,' I said, looking up into her face, 'is called Old Thundertits!'

Miss Webb did react, but not quite as obviously as the Misses Prowle.

In fact, she was really called Blackie, but when Arty was annoyed he used the other name.

I suppose it was a wicked thing to long for an air raid, but I did, and had to wait for three weeks for the siren to blow in school time.

It came one Wednesday, just after dinner time, and with instructions to go speedily home, class was abandoned. I set off down the road for the gate to Little Pant. Once inside the first field I slackened pace and scuffed delightedly through the long grass.

I was halfway across the second field when I saw her, Old Thundertits, lying on her side, all by herself.

She seemed such an odd shape, her stomach blown up

114

like a drum, and she was grunting great squirts of steam from her nose. I stood and watched for some minutes before I plucked up courage to draw closer.

Her one horn was covered in fresh soil where it had been digging in the ground and her eyes were stary and unblinking. It was only when I was very close that I noticed the lump under her tail. It was large and balloon-like and shimmered in the afternoon sun.

Every time she grunted it grew bigger, and when it suddenly moved, I held my breath.

I stood transfixed as the lump elongated, wriggled and writhed behind the old cow. Suddenly I was conscious of a droning in the air above, but I couldn't take my eyes off the swelling behind the straining legs. Old Thundertits was gasping, then the shape grew suddenly much bigger and the droning sound louder. For a fleeting second a great shadow covered us both, then there was a 'pop', the balloon burst and amid a rush of brown water I saw two small feet and a head appear. It was a baby calf.

Although I had never seen anything like it in my life before, I didn't feel frightened or ill – just mesmerized. Then the feet moved up and down as if waving at me and the mouth partly opened to give a watery bawling sound. Still moving its feet, it bawled again, then pushed out a short pink tongue that curled up to its nose.

I was in no doubt that the little creature was asking for help, so I squatted down and took hold of one of the legs with both hands.

I shall never forget the sensation. Warm and tacky it was, but it was a wonderful feeling of life, even though it was just a leg, which thrilled my whole tingling body.

The leg plucked back a shade, but I didn't let go. Then it came forward about six inches; I re-adjusted my squat and pulled gently, and the little creature came forward even more. Both legs were now clear to the shoulders and the head was quite free.

Suddenly, Old Thundertits gave one mighty heave and the calf shot halfway out, accompanied by a great flood that ran all around my boots. I stood up a little, and as I did there was another heave and out it came – all of it – wet and still bawling and its big brown eyes blinking in the light.

I stayed and watched the old lady get up and lick her newborn. It was unbelievable how quickly it tried to stand. I made a move to help but Old Thundertits moaned at me, so I left it alone.

It was only when the All-Clear sounded that I remembered about the air raid and, running through the cowpats, I sped home to tell Mother.

* * *

At that point, I drew my boyhood experience to a close. I stood there in the little schoolroom, with the evening sunshine shafting through the latticed windows, and to my surprise I sensed an air of expectancy – they wanted more!

No longer did I feel nervous or devoid of words. I was talking about what I knew and loved best, my life as a vet – and what was more, I was enjoying it.

So I carried on and told them how that incident instilled me with the wonderment of creation in the animal kingdom, and for me it was not a love of animals that drew me into my profession, for a sentimental love is no good to a vet, but rather it was respect. A respect for their instincts, whether aggressive or not, for in the main they were but natural reactions to threat, pain or for protection of their young. And a belief, too, that all creatures had a right to survive in God's World, in a way as conducive to their well-being, both mental and physical, as possible.

I discussed the university training, how vets over a period of five years accumulated the knowledge of animal anatomy and physiology; how disease affected the development and function of organs; how it could be best combated.

I talked of the importance of health control in livestock; how our work was divided into, firstly, the 'fire brigade' section, where emergencies such as calving cases, milk

116

fevers, horses with colic and accidents had to be attended immediately at any time of the night or day. Then the 'preventive' section, where an attempt was made to programme the control of parasites, mineral deficiencies, disease by vaccination and fertility.

I explained how pregnancy was detected in the dairy cow, regular conception being vital to the continued flow of milk. To me this feature of veterinary practice has always had a particular fascination, because to my knowledge, nobody else but a vet feels, with his hands, life developing at so early a stage.

The fact that it is done by rectal examination may seem distasteful to some; yet the minute one's fingers gently probe the uterine wall, feeling the membranes that surround the embryo, or even the tiny body itself as it bobs like a cork in the primeval lake that sustains it until birth, one cannot but marvel at the Grand Design of it all.

I talked about pets and their value in society; how they kept us sane in a confusing world with their loyalty, affection and companionship; and I talked of the heartache when they died, and the greater heartache and anguish of having to decide to put them to sleep. 'Calling it a day' before they reached the stage of indignity and suffering was difficult, for in a way we were being asked to play at being God, something which was beyond us. Yet it was one way of repaying years of unquestioned devotion on our pet's part.

I was honest about how I felt regarding field sports and told them what had led me to my present standpoint; I acknowledged how fortunate I was to be doing something I found so satisfying in the Herefordshire countryside and hoped that there would always be room for the country vet in society.

And I felt that there would be, as long as people enjoyed seeing horses like Kismet extending themselves in the beauty and grace of motion; were proud of raising fine livestock such as Herefords whose progeny, from stock improved by Master Breeders in the Borders, now populate the plains and prairies throughout the world; thrilled at sporting dogs who have their own beauty in action; or enjoyed the comfort and companionship of pets; and finally, as long as they needed a vet to explain some of the more delicate aspects of animal behaviour when necessary. After thanking them for being so kindly attentive, I finished.

And just like the time I had stood up in Class Two at Abergranog Council School all those years ago, to tell them about Old Thundertits and her calf, I went back to my seat amid the applause, feeling pretty pleased with myself.

Lady Octavia rose and thanked me profusely for a 'jolly fascinating chat', then asked for questions from the floor.

After an initial awkward silence they started to come and I answered queries on how to grow hair on guinea pigs, sexing guinea fowl and caring for orphan foxes, and I listened to several rather long but very charming personal experiences of pets and their habits.

Then there came a question from a dark-haired young woman, whom I had noticed during the evening to be attentive, yet without any sense of humour. When Lady Octavia asked for just one more, she stood up and, walking down the aisle a little way, faced me squarely. Shortish, with pale, pale features, her eyes were piercing and a trifle wild; in fact her whole appearance was rather ragged and windblown and she reminded me of the poem about 'Meg Merrillee', a wandering recluse who lived off nature.

'Yes, Lydia,' said Her Ladyship. 'What is your question to Mr Lasgarn?'

Lydia breathed in deeply and flushed a little:

'Madam Chairman,' she began, 'the speaker says – and I quote . . .' She looked down at a notepad on which she had recorded my words, something that took me a little aback. '"It is my belief that all creatures have a right to survive in God's world, in a way as conducive to their well-being, both mental and physical, as possible."'

She looked up at me with a questioning gaze and I nodded to confirm that it was what I had said; though I was a trifle surprised at the positiveness of my rhetoric.

'Why is it, then,' she said, tossing back strands of unkempt hair over her shoulders, 'why is it that you allow such iniquitous and barbaric enterprises as are to be established at Barrington, where animals will be incarcerated in a "Belsen"? How can you stand there and say that you care, when within three miles of where you live, animals will be imprisoned under conditions so inhumane that it is a disgrace to mankind? Your attitude of condoning such factory farming enterprises is not only hypocritical, but makes a mockery of your profession!' Then, before I could answer, she had turned, marched to the door, 'clacked' the latch and left.

A murmur of anxiety rippled through the other ladies, then Lady Octavia stepped in.

'I'm sorry about Lydia, Mr Lasgarn. She's a rather impetuous young lady – Vegan, you know. Please take no notice.'

'It's a pity I could not reply,' I said. 'She's quite entitled to her views.' But secretly I was glad I did not have to; for her question was a very real and disturbing one, something which, of course, I had not been unaware of in my career, and I was going to have to give an answer some time, if only to myself.

Following a proposal of thanks I was asked to judge the competition of 'Three Exciting Things To Do With A Wornout Feather Duster' of which some entries defied even the wildest of imaginations.

I drank several cups of tea and ate numerous sandwiches and cakes, bought a raffle ticket and won a knitted tea cosy donated by Dolly Pump, eventually arriving home at ten-thirty, feeling as if I had calved a hundred cows.

Di was anxious to know how I had got on and I gave her a brief resumé of the evening.

'You didn't say "THUNDERTITS" in front of all those women?' she gasped.

'Of course not, I called her Blackie,' I said. '. . . I think!'

The following day I drove about with a permanent grin on my face; after all, it was quite an achievement to keep thirty women amused, all at one time, and I felt I had done a good job.

'Any calls,' I shouted, as I walked in for lunch.

'Bayley's horse is still coughing. Stokes has got another dead sheep and Harry Payne wants some more of that "pink stuff" for his calves.' Then Diana appeared at the kitchen door. 'Lady Octavia rang to say how much your women all enjoyed it.'

'Good,' I said. 'That's nice.'

'Yes,' Diana continued, rather stonefaced. 'She said she thought Thundertits was "quaite a hoot".'

'Oh my God!' I said. 'I must have got carried away.'

'Sounds as if you did, my lad,' she went on. 'Lydia, whoever she is, rang and asked me to give a message to my "boss". She was sorry about last night and hoped you were not too upset by her performance.'

'Oh, Lydia.'

'Yes. L.Y.D.I.A.!'

'She was a girl I met . . .'

But Diana was already disappearing into the house, adding sharply, 'Your lunch is on the table.

I shook my head in despair.

'Two things I will never understand,' old Sam Juggins had once told me. 'Women and weather.'

Boy oh boy! Was he right!

8

Although I may have been a trifle carried away when I launched into the second phase of my talk to the Women's Institute, and despite the outburst from Lydia the Vegan, I meant what I said in relation to my belief that all creatures, man and animal alike, were entitled to live out their span in just fashion, subject of course to the demands of the balance of nature.

What of the welfare of the innocent baby rabbit sunning itself, when the hawk dives? Or the hens clustered together when the fox eases through the pen door? Or the jaws of the pike on the defenceless roach? Nature is cruel, yet who is to deny it is just?

For animals under our care – not just vets but anyone who has contact with their lives, from the blacksmith to the butcher – respect is what it is all about. From my own early experiences, however, I realized that it was not easy to bring satisfactory equality to the scene. Lydia the Vegan had put it straight: one was a hypocrite if one condoned exploitation of one's fellow creatures. Yet who could stand up and honestly say: 'I never did'? How could a country vet be at peace with himself and conform with the demands of society?

One was forced to take sides and sometimes in a most unintentional way: like stitching up gun-dogs ripped upon barbed wire, in order that they might continue to retrieve shot birds; or ministering to hunters, keeping them fit to carry their owners in pursuit of the fox; or even attending to animals like Lugg.

Lugg was jet-black, sleek, athletic, and belonged to Mrs Cornish. He had been born of a wild, scrawling, fleeting passion in the fields surrounding the village. Fathered by a wretched, battered tom of an innocent tortoiseshell mother, Lugg first caught the light of day in a local barn.

Captured and thrown into a brook to drown, he squeezed through a hole in the sack, was washed to the bank and, wet and bedraggled, staggered ashore. Mrs Cornish, a naturalist in her search of water flora, found him and took him in.

How she reared the sodden scrap is beyond imagination; she came to me and I advised her upon feeding and gave her some vitamin supplements to build up the strength of the tiny waif.

Lugg survived to become a fine cat.

Then one night, on the way home from a nocturnal sortie, he was in a collision with a car. Concussed and broken, he was brought to me: his eyes were full of haemorrhage, his ribs fractured, his body bruised; yet with surgical assistance and his owner's dedication, he survived.

It was some weeks later that I met Mrs Cornish in the village and enquired of Lugg.

She looked away and put her hand to her face.

My heart sank – he was dead.

'Far from it,' said Mrs Cornish. 'Lugg is very well indeed, but in disgrace.'

Seeing my perplexity, she explained. 'In our garden we have for the first time a nest of tree-creepers. Do you know what they look like . . . ?' Before I could answer she went on: 'Delicate, white-breasted, divine little beings . . . and to see them scampering up the bark is absolute wonderment.' She suddenly choked, then recovered. 'The chicks were so tiny . . . I was able to look at them just twice, for the parents were unbelievably attentive and I did not want to frighten them. It was such a happy family and I was so looking forward to them being a part of my garden.'

Her face hardened and she drew a deep breath.

'Then last Thursday Lugg found them and massacred the lot!' Mrs Cornish shook her head in anguish. 'I just do not understand it . . . after all we did for him.'

It was easy to be trite and say that Lugg was just

following his natural instincts as a hunter and that, heart-breaking as it was, he could not be held to blame; yet had he just been left to die following his accident, we humans would have been charged with cruelty. To be perfectly honest – like Mrs Cornish, I did not understand it either.

Man, as a higher being, has a social conscience and must accept responsibility for those less able, but not all higher things see it in the same light.

On one of my trips abroad concerning the Herefords, I had been sent to Morocco to discuss the importation of cattle to that country.

It was the first time I had visited that part of the globe and I do not think I have ever really recovered from the culture shock. It was just as if one was stepping backwards in time to biblical days, for the scenes in town and country, medinas and souks, were unforgettable, as was the poverty, the begging, the blindness and the disability.

And there is nothing more poignant than a dead Arab lying by a dead donkey, to illustrate the chasm between East and West.

I came upon him, or rather his pathetic bloodstained carcase, on the dusty, crumbling stretch of hardpacked earth that passed for the road from Marrakesh to Agadir. Away to the left lay the donkey, one pannier basket hanging loosely from the torn canvas girth. Despite the jerky spasm of a foreleg, the donkey was dead – and all around was fruit.

That was the odd thing: the man was crushed, the donkey badly mutilated . . . but the fruit, though scattered, was still whole. There were oranges, rich and luminous in the dust; bananas, grouped and single; bright peppers, aubergines and sad, irregular potatoes. Like a star exploded, a bag of saffron powder scarified the ground with yellow streaks, and coins, just three and small, lay wanting at the side.

The car, a faded green Estate, silent and twisted, stood upon the verge, its bonnet raised, engine steaming and windows shattered.

Around the scene the watcher, stood with silent concern, yet wary lest the wind of some responsibility drift their way. In little hooded groups, save for the ones that carried stones to mark the road, their ghoulish presence sent a shiver up my spine.

As the car pulled alongside, Ahmed, my driver, wound his window down and a peculiar mix of petrol, fruit and death wafted into my senses.

He called, in the sharp-edged Arabic lilt, courteous but forceful, as is their way. Faces appeared, bodies jostled to give the news, voices jabbered, hands raised, and Ahmed sifted through the panic-stricken chant to find reason.

As if to strangle the urgent babbling stream, he closed the window; though still the chatter filled the car until he had pulled well away.

'What an awful tragedy,' I said. 'They were all very upset.'

He nodded and replied, 'Yes. It was a good donkey.'

* * *

Some years later I was on holiday in Devon when, due to Bob Hacker's illness, the practice became shorthanded and I was forced to return to Ledingford, leaving Diana and the girls behind.

On the road from Sidford, I noticed a sign for the Donkey Sanctuary at Branscombe. It was only a minor detour and I had heard of the enterprise; though it had been rather unkindly described as a home for fleabitten mokes run by a rather cranky old lady.

The road took a pleasurable route along the fringe of the South Devon coast and eventually I came to a turning running down to Slade Farm – and all around were donkeys. Hundreds of them, happy, contented donkeys, and when I looked at the sign overhanging the gateway, I could see why. It read:

THE DONKEY'S CHARTER
This Charter grants every donkey admitted to this

Sanctuary the right of life, regardless of age or health, and to the best treatment, care and drugs to preserve its life to a maximum.

It grants permanent peace and freedom and when the time comes, a dignified and peaceful death.

Not far from my own sentiments; yet how was it, I wondered, in an age where battered babies, old folks, the sick and the destitute did not even appear to have such rights, that donkeys did?

I decided to find out and drove in; and what I discovered was quite a story.

Firstly the donkeys were not in any way 'fleabitten old mokes', for they were all in grand condition, glossy coated, alert and bright-eyed; and as for the description 'cranky old lady', of Elisabeth Svendsen who ran the sanctuary, nothing could have been more misleading.

Bright blonde and in her fifties, she was known as Mrs S and, straight away, the dynamism of her personality came forcefully through. Despite her Scandinavian looks and name, Elisabeth Svendsen was born a Yorkshire lass, trained as a teacher, then worked in her father's factory as a secretary and occasional heavy lorry driver. She married, brought up a family, including Sarah, her adopted and disabled daughter, as well as helping her husband create a successful manufacturing business.

Eventually selling the factory, the family moved to Devon, where they were able to indulge in their favourite hobby, sailing. Mrs S was a competent yachtswoman holding both navigational and radio certificates.

No 'cranky lady', no impetuous Vegan, no emotional misfit. Here was a woman leading a full and successful life – so why donkeys?

She answered me in one word. 'Humility,' she said. 'If donkeys were less humble and more reactionary, there would be no need for a sanctuary such as ours,' and although she admitted that much of the neglect resulted from ignorance rather than malice, she was able to quote some harrowing cases.

There were the 'Railway Donkeys', three 'pinks' or strawberry roans which became unwanted and were turned on to a railway track in the hope that the wheels of a fast train might solve the problem; Timothy, who had both ears lopped off by vandals; Gyppo, whose feet were torn and shoulders raw from hauling scrap metal over piles of used car bodies.

But in 1973 Elisabeth Svendsen's drive and dedication provided a sanctuary for such unfortunates, which today ranks as the fifth largest animal charity in the United Kingdom. It comprises four farms totalling 800 acres, a staff of 74 including two resident veterinary surgeons, and has more than 52,000 registered supporters.

Mrs S would be the first to admit that she never envisaged a 'donkey empire' when she started her small donkey stud; but a chance visit to Exeter market and the sight of seven emaciated, lice-infected donkeys crammed into a small pen, so horrified her that she dedicated herself to donkey welfare.

As her concern developed, she became known locally as the 'Donkey Lady' and her stud a haven for cases of cruelty and abuse. Such was the interest that support escalated and the Charity was formed.

Donations, gifts and legacies followed; one, however, caused quite a stir, for it was of considerable proportions, from a Miss Philpin of Reading, who for many years had been running her own Donkey Charity. On her death she left everything to Mrs Svendsen – no money, just a collection of outstanding bills and two hundred and four donkeys!

So developed the Charity as it stands today. Yet Mrs S's motivation for donkey welfare was not sentimental but intensely practical, for she did not confine her activities to donkeys in the Devon countryside, she travelled world-wide researching their conditions.

With the support of the Pfizer Company, who produce animal medicines, she initiated a programme for the eradication of parasites in donkeys; the effect of such control was dramatic and not only contributed to the welfare of the donkeys, but to their ability to work and improve the local economy. How different from the vociferous protests of some individuals and organizations who shout a lot and do little; to me Elisabeth Svendsen's approach was a true application of animal welfare.

Nor did she neglect the veterinary care of her donkeys at home. 'Health Makes for Happiness' was her maxim and was aptly portrayed in the veterinary facilities she had installed.

The hospital at first seemed to me over-indulgent, when one considered the financial constraints on the National Health Service; but their vet, John Fowler, put things in perspective.

'As a welfare organization we do not undertake research,' he explained. 'However, we are able to keep records of all tests and treatments and have built up a good pattern of clinical data, not just for the benefit of the donkeys, but for other species including man himself. In fact,' he added, 'we are now one of the main centres for information in the world and recently I have been to North Africa advising on donkey health. There is a move to set up "night clinics" in Sudan and Ethiopia, where working donkeys can receive attention and be rested if not fit, the owner being loaned another in its place – a chain of facilities, of practical as well as humanitarian value to both man and beast.'

I was fascinated by the whole enterprise and so glad I had called. But there was an even more intense revelation to come as well as caring for the donkeys, collecting clinical data and giving foreign aid, Mrs Svendsen's most rewarding achievement came from a visit to the Sanctuary by a small party of handicapped children.

'The reaction was so wonderful,' she said, her eyes lighting with pleasure. 'They all found so much joy in cuddling the donkeys, who seemed to enjoy it, too. And when they rode, it was as if a newfound energy surged through their flaccid bodies – and they laughed and gurgled with joy. You just wouldn't believe it.'

Oh, I would, Mrs Svendsen, I thought, as the word 'humility' echoed in my ears.

For it was my turn to feel humble. Humble and rather ashamed, as memories of Abergranog Park and Daft Lenny filtered through my mind.

* * *

It was the day that Boxy Potter had pinched the bottle of cider from his Uncle Idwal's pub. We were all sitting in the Shelter swigging it; there was Boxy, me, Wendel Weekes and Dicky Trimble.

The Shelter was an open-fronted building in Abergranog Park where we met to hatch out our plots: evil little doings such as catching bumble bees in matchboxes, then letting them out in the Capitol Cinema where they would cause quite a commotion before flying on to the screen. Or there was the time we switched all the seed packets on the allotments, causing much consternation amongst the old men when their carrots came up looking like lettuce and their broccoli like onions.

It was the place we met when we cut Band of Hope, where Mr Talfyn Thomas lectured us on the evils of strong drink – not that his tirades against the 'devil's brew' were having much effect.

It was the first time I had ever tasted cider. Although it was bitter, and drinking out of the flagon caused the bubbles to come back through my nose, I did not dislike it.

We passed the bottle about, wiping the neck with our grimy hands before drinking as we had often seen the men doing. The effect on our youthful systems was quite potent and before long we were laughing, joking and arguing with great gusto.

I had been telling them about the gymkhana at Pontypool Park where I had seen Colonel Harry Llewellyn on a horse called Foxhunter, little realizing how famous the pair were to become.

'I could do that,' said Boxy, lifting the bottle, 'if I 'ad a 'orse!'

128

'You can't ride,' said Wendel, who though normally timid had found a new confidence.

'Course I can, I can ride like a cowboy if I want to,' said Boxy, for he was more than just a romantic, he was a downright liar at times.

'You couldn't even ride Ben Hatcher's donkey,' said Wendel, going further than ever he had done in a confrontation with the toughest member of our group.

At that point, Daft Lenny arrived on the scene.

I never ever knew what his proper name was, though he had been about for as long as I could remember. He lived somewhere at the top of the village in the Fifteen Houses, a long row of terraced dwellings built on such a slope that it was often said the people who lived there had one leg longer than the other.

He was difficult to age, and though he didn't look it, he must have been a bit older than the rest of us, for he was dressed in grown-up clothes – long baggy trousers, jacket with the sleeves obscuring his hands, and always an open-necked khaki shirt and sandals. Winter or summer, freezing or boiling, Daft Lenny always wore the same.

His body was short and squat and he walked or trotted mostly in a disjointed amble, his head nodding loosely upon his shoulders; but it was his features that were the most odd, for his forehead was equal in size to the rest of his face and topped by a round patch of ginger hair.

To us Lenny was just daft; to the medical men he was a 'cretin'.

He was neither ignored nor accepted, just tolerated; though occasionally the kids would bait him and he would chase them around the Park, waving his arms in the air and sweating profusely.

There was a rhyme they used to chant, that in itself adds a peculiar significance to the whole story:

> Lenny is a donkey,
> Donkeys eat the grass,
> Come and chase us, donkey
> And kick us up the arse!

When excited, Lenny would gurgle and grunt, but when calm he could pronounce some words and make himself partly understood.

When he saw our bottle he asked for a drink.

'Shove off, Len,' said Boxy.

'Give him some,' said Wendel, now a man and a half. 'Give him a drink!'

'Go on,' said Dicky and I in unison.

So Boxy gave Daft Lenny a drink and we carried on with our conversation.

Wendel fished inside his trouser pocket and brought out a little cloth bag, closed by a noose. It contained his glass alleys.

Wendel may have been a bit of a weed – though after a few gulps of cider he was certainly different – but he was a superb marble player and within the bag were his three 'Bobs'; champion 'Bobs' at that.

Like a gambler in a western saloon and equal in his romanticism to Boxy's cowboy allusion, he chucked them down on the floor.

Had he said, 'I'll see yer, Tough Guy!' it would have matched.

But he didn't. He just said:

'Them to yer sheath knife, you bloody can't!'

That was some challenge, for Boxy's sheath knife was legendary. It had been used by Boxy's Uncle Idwal when he had escaped from Colditz; there was still the blood of the German General that Boxy's Uncle Idwal had used as hostage when he walked through the lines of guns as he crossed the frontier, and when they shot, they killed the General who fell back on the knife that Boxy's Uncle Idwal was holding to make him walk.

That very same knife had been the one that had cut the rope releasing the barge that drifted down the river into the Brumaagen power station, which blew half of the German Navy to bits when it went.

It was the knife given to Boxy's Uncle Idwal by a Russian Count, dying of exposure on the icefield, whom Uncle Idwal had dragged when the sled dogs died of exhaustion.

And the knife Uncle Idwal had given to Boxy.

An awe-inspiring thing; and how amazing that you could buy replicas of it in Bennet's Army Stores in Newpool.

Boxy was visibly shaken. Firstly by the audacity of little Wendel, yet it was his fault for giving him the 'devil's brew'; secondly, because despite its doubtful authenticity, it was a good-looking knife and Boxy did not want to part with it; and thirdly because he had never had his bum on a horse's back in his life.

But Boxy was supposed to be tough and Wendel weak; Dicky and me watched him closely and enjoyed seeing him squirm.

'My knife and his Bobs; Lasgarn, you put in your cards, and, Trimble, your fags.' Dicky Trimble was the only one who smoked. 'An' whoever stays on 'im the longest, gets the lot!'

That took the smile off my face and Dicky nearly got up and left.

'Come on,' said Boxy to me. 'You seen that Fox'unter, so you'm in it as well.'

My cards were a tiny set of playing cards, miniatures that I had bought for twopence at a jumble sale for the Missionary Fund; I did not play cards and did not really know why I bought them, but they seemed to hold a peculiar fascination for my pals and were highly prized.

Even then I felt that if it was anything to do with animals, I ought to be able to cope; though, like Boxy, I had never had my bum on a horse, I took out my little pack of cards in their tattered cover and placed them next to Wendel's 'Bobs'.

Dickie took out his packet of five 'Loadstone', a make I've never heard of since, and put them on the pile.

Boxy made a pretence that he could not get the knife off his belt, to which Wendel boldly remarked, 'Put the bloody belt in as well.'

After that it soon became detached.

'Shake!' said Wendel.

So we all stood over the pile of wagers and shook hands.

'Right,' continued Wendel, 'I seen Ben Hatcher in the village as I come up. He'll be doin' his shopping, an' then be in the Crown for a bit. We'll go now!'

So out of the Shelter we trooped.

'Go home, Lenny,' said Boxy harshly. 'This en't for nut'eads!' Lenny made some noises indicating he wanted to come, but Boxy ran at him, waving his arms, shouting, 'Scram off!'

And Lenny reluctantly went.

We had gone but a hundred yards when Wendel's bravado took a turn for the worse. He went green, felt sick and raced back to the lavatory; then Boxy wanted a pee and so did I, so we all went.

Ben Hatcher was a bit of a recluse who lived on a patch of common land that ran alongside the Avon Llwyd with his half-dozen cats, a German Shepherd called Twm, and his donkey.

It was just on one o'clock when we arrived at his patch, ready to put ourselves to the test. Along the way we had collected a cabbage, which Dicky said donkeys liked, and he was quite confident that it would attract Ben's moke.

He was called Harold and was quite old, and it was said he had been rescued from ill treatment at the seaside by some Chapel people and Ben had offered to look after him.

Scruffy in appearance, with a grey, fleabitten, shaggy coat, pot-belly, a grizzled muzzle and white spectacles, Harold's movements were restricted by a long rope that ran from his tattered head collar to a tree. Despite the restraint, he was able to graze a wide area, all the while swishing his tail irritably as he picked at the clumpy grass.

When we got to the gate, he looked up curiously for a few moments, then gave a rather supercilious snort and returned to his grazing.

'Show 'im 'ewer cabbage, Dick,' said Boxy, pushing Dicky to the fore.

Brandishing the stolen bait aloft like an Olympic torch, Dick advanced.

''Old it down, 'ew twt!' shouted Boxy. 'What d'ew think it is, a camel?'

Dicky lowered the cabbage and nervously moved towards Harold, who surprisingly enough showed a decided interest in the offering. In fact it worked a treat and Dicky, full of confidence now that his idea had proved a success, took hold of the head collar and beckoned us.

'Come on, boys, it's safe now,' he shouted. 'I got 'im tight.'

'Right,' said Boxy, boldly. 'My go first. Give us a leg up, Lasgarn.'

So with Dicky Trimble holding his head collar and Wendel keeping a lookout, I took hold of Boxy's left leg and heaved. He went up all right, but disappeared over the other side instantaneously, being deposited in an ungainly heap on the floor.

Castigating me for 'legging' him too hard, he made a second attempt. This time he managed to get seated; but only for a fleeting second before Harold dropped his muzzle to take a bite of the cabbage which Dicky had let fall to the floor, pitching Boxy again into a heap in front of him.

Blazing away this time at Dicky, he clambered aboard once more and, when settled, shouted for the head collar to be released. However, when it was, nothing happened; and despite Boxy's urgings, Harold just stood like a statue.

In desperation Boxy dug his heels into Harold's flabby flank, at which point the old donkey, with the full benefit of his seaside experience, gave a wicked flip with his hindquarters and deposited his rider in a bunch of nettles.

Boxy retired hurt and my turn followed.

Being of a somewhat innovative nature, I tied the shank of the rope over Harold's withers to act as reins.

Boxy, sore and stinging from the nettles, proclaimed I was cheating, but had to admit it was a pretty 'horsey' thing to do.

I mounted, took the reins and shouted, 'Ceem-up, Harold!'

Harold took two paces forward and sportingly gave a repeat performance of his seaside acrobatics; the next thing

I knew I was landing hard upon my left elbow, my face impressed in a fresh pile of donkey droppings.

Wendel attempted to back out, saying he was still feeling sick; but we all insisted he should take part.

He approached Harold in such a state of nervousness that he frightened the donkey as well, to such effect that Harold lashed out and kicked Wendel on the knee.

Dicky Trimble thought it was a huge joke, until Harold bit his ear and made it bleed.

'Let me 'ave the bugger,' said Boxy, who had cut a stick from the hedge with his prized knife; but before he could grab the halter, Harold had turned about and kicked him right in the crutch, flooring him in agony.

Then, after looking around defiantly as if to say, 'Any more for any more?' he gave a superior guffaw and trotted out through the gate we had thoughtlessly left open, to disappear up the lane.

'Now we'em for it,' exclaimed Dicky. 'Old 'Atcher'll kill us!'

'We'd better go and catch him,' I said.

'I'm goin' 'ome,' moaned Boxy, rubbing his private parts gingerly, 'that donkey 'urt me.'

'An' me,' added Wendel, limping up to us.

My arm was aching right up to the shoulder, Dick's ear was still bleeding profusely and so, like walking wounded, we set off up the lane.

We had just rounded the first bend when our injuries suddenly became of secondary importance, for coming toward us was none other than old Ben Hatcher himself.

The lane was high-sided, giving no chance for escape, and retreat was an obvious admission of guilt; so we stopped in our tracks until Ben Hatcher confronted us.

'Now 'ere be a fine lookin' sight, Twm,' said Ben to the lean German Shepherd, who snarled between his teeth aggressively. 'Wonder what they been doin' down at my place?'

'Someone let your donkey out, Mr Hatcher,' I volunteered. 'And we'em lookin' for it.'

'Now there be a kind thing to do.' Then he took a quick

step forward and caught me by the jersey and, in a haze of beer fumes that nearly keeled me over, rasped; 'An' who let 'im out then, tell me that?'

'Daft Lenny!' said Boxy. ''E did it!'

'Is that so?' said Ben Hatcher, screwing up my jersey even tighter.

'Yes,' I said weakly. And Wendel and Dicky nodded in agreement.

I knew it was wrong to take advantage of Lenny. How selfish one can be when one's own skin is at stake.

Ben Hatcher released his grip and stood back, surveying us with a mean gaze.

'Well, I think you'm a bunch of liars,' he said. 'For I just seen Lenny, an' he was a'lookin' for you! Now 'ew boys tell me the truth or I'll let Twm 'ave a go, an 'e ain't had 'is dinner yet!'

As if Twm knew exactly what his master had said, he stepped forward menacingly and the explanation tumbled out of our mouths like a mountain stream.

'Wager, eh!' said Ben Hatcher, when we had finished. 'Well, I'll give you another one. I'll wager unless you gets my donkey back in this field and tied up in 'alf an 'our, I'll 'ave you down the cop shop, afore you can say "Yanto". Understand?'

We nodded. 'Let'em by, Twm,' he ordered, 'they got work to do.'

Having nervously skirted the slobbering jaws, we were about to set off in pursuit of the escapee when we had the shock of our lives, for coming towards us at a steady pace was Harold himself, and sitting on top quite sedately, with a joyous smile upon his face, was Daft Lenny.

'Well done, Lenny!' 'Good boy, Lenny!' 'Smashin', Lenny!'

Our cries of relief went up in unison as the pair approached, and Harold made no attempt to shy or kick at the outburst. How Lenny had managed to catch the flighty little donkey and mount him after our performance was a complete mystery; yet whatever, there was Harold seeming so calm and content that it was almost unbelievable, as did Lenny in a way that was rather uncanny.

Mercifully, it appeared we were off the hook; but Ben Hatcher was not yet finished with us. When they pulled up alongside, he took hold of Harold's collar.

'Thank you, Lenny my boy,' he said, patting his donkey's scraggy neck. 'One o' you is worth this lot put together.' Then he rubbed his stubbly chin and a gleam came into his eye. 'I do believe that there's a few prizes goin' for the best donkey rider, an' I would say that you'm about won 'em. What do 'ew say, boys?'

What could we say? And we sheepishly nodded our agreement.

"And 'em over to Lenny,' ordered Ben Hatcher.

And one by one we offered up our prized possessions – Wendel's 'Bobs', Dicky's Loadstone fags, Boxy's Uncle Idwal's knife and my pack of miniature playing cards. Each of us stepped forward in turn – and each time Daft Lenny smiled and shook his head.

'Don' you want any of it?' asked Ben Hatcher. Lenny smiled and grunted, then urged Harold forward. 'I . I . I . uunn . . onkey,' he burbled. 'Uuun . . onkey.'

'An' so you shall, Lenny my boy,' said Ben Hatcher, having interpreted the words. 'You can ride Harold any time you likes; as for all that old rubbish, fags, knives, cards and marbles, you'm quite right to refuse it. There's only one place for that, in the river.' And he held out his hand and collected them all.

Boxy was walking about like a cripple for quite some time and Wendel was about the same; Dicky had to have two stitches in his ear and I had suffered a 'greenstick' fracture in my fall and had my arm encased in plaster of Paris for six weeks.

Whatever the others learned from that I do not know, but the episode made a deep and lasting impression upon me. It was a humbling experience to find that a simple boy like Daft Lenny had achieved something we had failed to do, and when he was offered our prize possessions, he refused them; refused them graciously, without condescension or malice, even though we had originally tried to blame him – though of that he was blissfully unaware. It made the whole experience the more poignant in the memory

* * *

So when Elisabeth Svendsen described her relationship with the handicapped children and their unique rapport with her donkeys, I did know something about it and I did understand.

She, being the resourceful person that she was, had decided to develop this bond and had set up the Slade Centre for Handicapped Children. There were many objections, but she was not to be beaten and, after two years of tenacious lobbying, eventually planning permission was granted and the Slade Centre built. In the unit was a riding arena, play area, special toilets, medical room, kitchen and stables for the donkeys to be petted.

Parties of disabled children were fetched every day in the Charity's 'Blue Bus', and as I left it passed me; odd little faces at the windows. Some saw me and waved; others gazed beyond; yet all in their own way radiated complete happiness, just as Lenny had done on that day in the lane in Abergranog.

Like the donkeys, they had much in common: often misunderstood, sometimes unwanted and rejected; but then, thanks to Elisabeth Svendsen and her unique approach to animal welfare, at least the donkeys had a Charter and that was their good fortune. But a donkey is too humble an animal to covet good fortune, so it was sharing it with those little handicapped mites down at Slade Farm.

Just as Harold did for many years with Lenny.

9

As well as keeping an eye on my comings and goings at Gatewood from the tower of Welbury Church, the Little Owl had an admirable view of the whole village and the surrounding countryside.

What a contrast to Abergranog, where the best view was from the top of the Pentwyn Tips – a large elevated peninsula of slag waste, the by-product of the British Iron Works, long since defunct.

My life had seen a great contrast in geographical terms, even though, as the crow flies, I was living no more than fifty miles from where I was born; the salient difference being that I was now on the other side of the mountain, amongst the lush watermeadows and pastures of Herefordshire.

Here the harvests for years had been corn, apples, hops and fat cattle; but in the valleys there was just one product that had fed and nurtured the communities – 'glc'.

For 'glo' is coal and in my youth, though Abergranog lay on the fringe of the mining industry, the years of toil and tragedy, of oppression and exploitation by mine masters and industrialists to harvest the 'black diamond', had left their mark not only upon the landscape, but upon the character of the people as well.

Often when I sat with my father in the bottom-aching pews of High Street Baptist Chapel, as the Reverend Deri Jones communicated with the Almighty, my eyes would wander along the plaques and tablets that bedecked the walls, commemorating local worthies and their families.

Of all the elaborate designs, the one that held my gaze longer than any was a white marble slab in the fashion of the front elevation of a Greek Temple, with pillars at either side and a sloping façade at the top. Below, in stark black lettering, it read:

In Memory of those killed in the Llanerch Pit
Explosion, February 6th, 1890.
One hundred and seventy-six men and boys who
perished on that day.

What a grandiose epitaph compared with their earthly abode, where whole streets of 'one-up-one-downs' lost husbands and sons, some just children of ten years old, in the tragedy which occurred at 8.30 a.m. on 6 February, just as the colliery had been two hours into full work.

The underground district involved was called Cook's Slope in the Meadow Vein, where the workings had been opened up within the previous three years and were in the course of extension. Only the examiner who did the initial test for the highly inflammable methane used a safety lamp, the rest of the miners lighting their way with naked flames.

Thus it was that the treacherous gas, 'firedamp' as it was termed in mining parlance, was ignited to cause the explosion.

At the inquest, Mr Martin, the Inspector of Mines, reported that the point of ignition had been fixed at the horse windway of No. 4 Level. Also that there was an ignition of firedamp from a naked light used there by the men who were repairing the way, and that the area of the explosion was materially extended by dust and pockets of gas in the small cavities that were impossible to check with a safety lamp.

There had been no grounds for thinking that there were any accumulations of gas in the mine that morning. The examiner reported none, and maintained at the inquest that he failed to see any trace of gas; though he admitted there were some finished stalls on No. 1 level on the outbye side of the cross cut from No. 2, which he did not examine; nor had he done so for some days, as he did not consider they required it.

'Whatever duties or actions he may have omitted or

committed improperly,' said Mr Martin in mitigation, 'he gave his evidence in a credible and straightforward manner and I have no reason to suspect the truthfulness of it.'

Yet despite this statement, the poor man carried the major burden of responsibility, whereas the true negligence lay higher up.

'The owners had been pressed by me for some time previous to the explosion to introduce safety lamps as a precaution, as is the standard practice in many other mines. I received a promise from the Managing Director that they would do so gradually, but as the result shows,' said Mr Martin sadly in conclusion, 'it was not done in time.'

There was an ever constant stream of fatalities in Abergranog in those days, coupled with injuries, maimings and lung diseases associated with inhalation of coal dust.

A fund was set up for the widows, of ten shillings a week, and all widows received a Bible from the British and Foreign Bible Society. Religion, like a good cup of tea, was a great source of comfort for many and its seeds, sown on the field of human tragedy, germinated readily as the Great War followed in 1914 and cut down even more of the valley's young men.

When the senseless carnage had subsided and Taffy came marching home, in a few years there was the General Strike that brought poverty of even greater proportions. Children went to school with no stockings, and shoes from which the toes had been worn away. Inspections for new shoes took place, and there was the tale of Mr Sidney Griffiths, the School Boss, who heard that a father had sold his son's new allocation in the local pub. Down he went, gave the man a severe hiding, recovered the shoes and returned them to the child – rough, but honest justice.

Food was brought from the soup kitchens to schools in zinc baths for the needy – when they attended, and were not press-ganged by their parents into 'picking the tips' for coal.

Then to cap it all, there was an outbreak of smallpox.

* * *

When I was born in the early thirties, things had improved somewhat, but the character of the folks of Abergranog, moulded by the events of the previous decades, was in some way imprinted upon me and will forever leave its trace.

Of course, it is only in later years, when one is given to a degree of retrospection, that one realizes the influences of youthful days, for at that time we trod the directed pathways with little heed for betterment.

My Baptist upbringing was no stricter than that of any other of my pals; attendance was the main prerequisite and more important than indoctrination – as long as you went, it was all right.

And so I went three times on Sunday and once a week to Band of Hope, where we learned about drinking.

The Sunday services I found boring, except when there was a baptism by total immersion. On such an occasion the floorboards were removed from the deacon's dais to reveal a little swimming pool in which the Reverend Deri, clad in a gown weighted to prevent it floating up, and fisherman's waders, would carry out the ceremony in grand style.

To the elders, Chapel was a very serious affair, even though the Nonconformist element of Presbyterians, Wesleyans, Congregationalists and Baptists was less formal than High Church.

Of course there were some bright occasions, such as the day my cat Boggy turned up during the sermon and pounced on the artificial bird that the younger Miss Prowle, the organist, wore upon her hat; or the time we astounded the congregation with our verses.

There was a point during morning service when the Reverend Deri would devote a few minutes to the younger generation, prefacing his remarks by asking for quotations from the Bible. There were some kids who gloried in being able to spout great tracts of the Good Book, putting the rest of us to shame.

When the great man's finger pointed in your direction, something had to be produced. If you were lucky to get in first you could use 'Jesus wept', the shortest verse in the Bible, but they didn't like it because they thought it was cheating.

One Sunday the Reverend Deri made some cutting remarks about those of us whose repertoire was rather limited, saying that he would expect better next time. It was Boxy Potter's idea and the following week we made a very special effort. There was Boxy, Wendel and me, not sitting all together, but scattered about the body of the Chapel with our parents.

When the time came we were ready. Boxy got up first and in his husky voice pronounced from the *Book of Job*:

'"The meat in his bowels hath turned; he hath swallowed down riches and shall vomit them up; and God will cast them out of his belly."'

The Reverend Deri gave a cough, nodded and Boxy, with a satisfied smile, sat down.

Then came Wendel:

'*Deuteronomy*. Chapter twenty-seven. Verse twenty-three,' he piped up. '"Cursed is he that lieth with his mother-in-law. And all the people shall say, Amen."'

The Reverend Deri's face came over glazed and a quite audible 'ooh!' erupted from the younger Miss Prowle, behind the organ screen.

Recovering, the Reverend Deri rubbed his hands together ominously, the suspicion of a conspiracy beginning to dawn upon him.

'Hugh Lasgarn!' he said, and an air of anticipation filled the Chapel.

'"He that sinneth in such a way shall be cast out, having his privy member cut off and thrown to the beasts."'

It was not quite as it was written, but it did the trick.

The following week, the Reverend Deri decided to have no verses and told us a story instead.

However, Chapel was not all that bad, for there was the Anniversary tea, followed by Sports on Mrs Williams' tennis court, with ice-cream and toffees as prizes. Then there was the outing to Barry Island every year and the Christmas Party in the schoolroom.

But on Sundays it was Chapel in the morning, Sunday School in the afternoon and Chapel at night, with a walk through the Trevethin Wood afterwards in summer and home to ham salad with cold green peas, my favourite.

What a contrast in style and belief are the religions of the world: the very buildings themselves give token to it and even exaggerate it by virtue of their age and design. Temples, mosques, cathedrals and lofty rural spires as in Welbury, all reaching for the Heavens in glorification.

Yet if anything, in Abergranog it was the Pentwyn Tips that in a way acted as a surrogate tower; for if the monks brought religion to Welbury in the thirteenth century, it was the British Iron Works that was instrumental in bringing it to my home valley 500 years later, for it was they who built the church.

With the works came the workers, and Abergranog suddenly became heavily populated. In 1840 the population was some 8000 souls, in contrast to Welbury's 400. There were five per cent Irish, with slightly less English than Welsh, most of the latter speaking only their native tongue.

The Irish, many of whose descendants still live in the valley today, built the Roman Catholic Church, whilst chapels sprouted like mushrooms, bearing the severe biblical Welsh names of Noddfa, Pisgah and Siloh.

In contrast, whilst the tentacles of the Industrial Revolution were creeping into the Welsh hillsides, in Welbury, local industries of basket-making, weaving, silkwinding, cheese-making, glove- and nail-making were being killed off.

Whilst the blast furnaces of Abergranog threw out their devilish heat, tinting the ragged horizons as they lit up the night sky and extruding mile upon mile of railway lines, by peculiar contrast, the business of nail-making in Welbury was in decline and the long, straight, smallheaded nails, so popular with undertakers, were eventually to be made no more.

Likewise, the watch and clockmaker was repairing

instead of making; the tallow chandlers imported their dips; the blacksmith did the work of the cooper and the wheelwright, as well as his own.

Welbury no longer brewed its famous ale: 'Oh, the mutability of human affairs!' exclaimed a leader writer in the *Ledingford Journal* of 1871, when the news was announced.

What a decline in fortune for such a place that in its time had been an ancient borough town and parish, had been fought over in many skirmishes and wars and had even, prior to the Reform Act of 1832, returned two Members of Parliament.

At a time when the main streets of Welbury were described as being 'ankle-deep in mud and furrowed as if by a plough-share', just across the river and the mountain ranges there were roads and railways, inclines, tramways and canals – all geared to the coal and iron harvest.

If, by comparison, the rural scene still appeared pleasant and peaceful, certainly the names of the farms and fields did much to reflect it – such dreamy spots as Rushy Meadow, Little Harbour Leys, Muskberry Piece and Shady Banks. In Abergranog, it was pits and ponds that gave titles to the area: Balance Pit, Ladder Pit, Hole-in-the-Field, Kay's Slope or the Harmonium, a pit so called because most of the miners had small musical organs in their homes.

There was the Red Ash; idyllic in sound and idyllic in being if in Welbury; but in Abergranog it was a hellhole and the worst of the mines, where the seams were low, water waist-deep and many men contracted pneumoconiosis, a vicious disease caused by inhalation of dust and damp that rotted their lungs and clawed at their straining hearts.

Then there was the Llanerch, ironically when translated into Welsh the most pastoral of all: it means the 'Glade'.

Armageddon came in the form of the collapse of the ironworks; railway tracks were converted to steel and the populace was on the move once again. Abergranog, like

Welbury, was in a state of decay; what was left was but a shell.

Yet there was a difference, for though resident for a relatively short time in the valley, the nationalities stamped a cosmopolitan marque upon the religion and politics in a manner which influenced deeply the character of future generations. Generations like my own, who never forgot the stranglehold society had had upon their forebears and determined it should never happen to them.

For this reason, maybe, together with a degree of hybrid vigour initiated by a mix of bloods, in due course the sons and daughters of Abergranog graced the professions, the arts and politics and became pioneers and settlers throughout the world.

By contrast, from Welbury the greatest ambassadors were the descendants of the white-faced cattle whose bloodlines had been developed and improved within five miles of Welbury Church, by the legendary Tomkins family, yeoman farmers and grand stockmen. Their cattle, too, went to countries afar, but the character and physique of the magnificent beasts had resulted from careful breeding and not the vagaries of social environment.

How strange to ponder that there must be Welshmen farming Herefords abroad, both, human and animal, descended from stock which started life just fifty miles apart.

Abergranog, where I spent my youth, where my sensitivities and outlook were moulded in many ways by the sombre happenings of the industrial past; and now Welbury, my home: the fresh country air, rural peace, animals . . . and, of course, their owners. A tale of two villages.

Yet, whatever the community, the pattern of the relationship of man and woman to creatures, whether food animals or pets, says much for the spirit of that society.

* * *

I shall never forget my first Hereford Bull Sale, for a very special reason.

They were always most prestigious affairs, the Ascot of the cattle world, where nobility rubbed shoulders with breeders and buyers, and Stetson-hatted Canadians, po-faced Russians, swarthy Latins and flamboyant Americans added international flavour. With more than two hundred bulls offered, there was worldwide interest, and quality Herefords were highly sought, their ability to acclimatize readily in diverse terrain and climate enhancing the demand.

Ledingford Market was transformed into a tented village, the starkness of brick and metal softened by bright awnings and banners over bars and eating places.

The bulls came in on Sunday night, some having travelled from as far afield as the north of Scotland. Each had a pen and number allocated, around which the paraphernalia of showing and selling was assembled: massive stock boxes, buckets, brushes, combs and cloths; snow-white linen halters and shining leather collars, their brass buckles glinting merrily in the abundant lights.

Even at that early stage, an air of competition already pervaded the animal-warm atmosphere, the excitement accentuated by the constant lowing of the bulls and the urgent chatter of their human counterparts.

The Show was held on the Monday. In turn, the Champions of each class were selected, leading up to the climax in late afternoon, when the Supreme Champion, the Bull of the Show, was chosen. Cups and trophies were presented at the Herd Book Supper, held that evening in the Green Dragon, and a sumptuous affair it was, too. Then on Tuesday came the Grand Sale, with bulls and money changing hands publicly and privately.

It was all quite a do.

As veterinary surgeons to the Society, our job was to ensure that every bull was fit and healthy, free from infectious or contagious disease, in good bodily condition and showing no signs of hereditary weakness or deformity.

Such bulls were to be the foundation of many a new herd and would dictate the quality of future progeny. The bull is half the herd, it was said, and if the true characteristics as originally envisaged by the Tomkins were to be handed on, standards had to be maintained.

Each class was made up of bulls of a similar age and was brought in turn to an area behind the main ring. Here, away from the hustle and bustle of the Showyard, the animals were led around one at a time so that an examination of their action could be made and any lameness, leg weakness or hip abnormality detected.

Then followed a closer examination, starting from the tip of the nose through to the end of the tail.

Nostrils clean, eyes bright with no discharge from either. Teeth level with the leading edge of the upper hard palate or dental pad; this latter feature was extremely important, for any deviation fore or aft was described as over- or under-shot and could impair the grazing action considerably. If this bad character was passed on, whole herds could suffer the consequences and be poor 'do-ers' as a result.

A hand over the shoulders and down the forelegs detected any joint enlargement and was concluded with a visual examination of the claws of the feet to ensure they were sound and even. Then the underside of the belly; hind limbs; tail and finally testicles – a vital part of the whole examination: full development, even size and freedom from adhesions were the requirements.

A final appraisal of skin and coat; then it was 'Good Luck' to the handler and on with the next.

My involvement came as a result of Bob Hacker being taken ill, leaving me in sole charge of the veterinary examination.

It was a crisp, bright morning and the bulls seemed sharpened by the frosty air. They were a good bunch and the organization excellent, such that by eleven o'clock I was over half-way through.

Paxton had two entries: a smart little yearling called Donhill Button and a much larger companion called Groucho. I had noticed the old man standing a little way

147

off, tapping his silver-topped cane whilst I checked them over; not overtly intimidating, but just letting me know he was about.

In fact there had been little of which to complain, and I was enjoying seeing so many grand cattle parading, just for me.

The trouble came in the form of a bull called Duncalm Folk Hero, a powerful animal with a rich mahogany coat that glistened in the wintry sun.

The stockman, a bearded individual in a white smock and hat, walked him around. Folk Hero's action was smooth and confident, holding his head proudly and tugging just occasionally on the nose lead, as if to show who was really the boss.

I pulled him in for the detailed examination and all was well until I ran my hand down the left side of his neck: just where the red hair merged with the white, I noticed some circular bald patches. They had been dusted with chalk and the hair combed across, yet the more I looked, the more obvious they became.

Without comment I carried on and when I came to the tailhead I discovered more such circular patches, though this time they had been darkened with a brown powder.

Further close scrutiny of the skin showed several similar lesions and I came to the conclusion the bull was suffering from ringworm. The condition was contagious and as such was not acceptable; Duncalm Folk Hero would have to be turned out.

'Ringworm!' spluttered the stockman. 'Bloody rubbish! 'E's been rubbing on the rails, that's all. Got overheated with his feed.'

'In my opinion it is ringworm,' I told him, firmly. 'And under Society rules, I cannot let this bull go forward.'

He pulled Folk Hero's head round and came close to me.

'Society rules, eh!' he hissed. 'This bull belongs to Mr Chuffington.'

'I can see that from the catalogue,' I said. 'Now on you go!'

I made a note of my findings and, after washing up, carried on with my examinations; but it was not long before Gerald Wilbert, the Society secretary, arrived, decidedly agitated.

'The bull with ringworm,' he said, in a manner rather like a spy passing on a message, 'Are you sure?' I nodded my confirmation. 'Going to cause a bit of a stink.' He looked about, again in a distinctly clandestine manner. 'Belongs to Mr Chuffington, you know.'

'Yes,' I said, 'I do know. What difference does that make?'

'Well, nothing, I suppose,' he groaned, 'except that he has just been elected President of the Society and that bloody bull was in line for the Championship!'

Lasgarn's Luck! Two hundred bulls and the first one I sling out belongs to the President.

Wilbert huffed, puffed, then scurried off, and I tried to concentrate on the job in hand; but within minutes he was back again.

'He is pretty upset,' he said breathlessly. 'He wants to have a word with you, down at the office.'

I looked around: there were three bulls left.

'I will come after this Class,' I said. 'But the bull has to go.'

'Oh, I know! I know!' wailed Wilbert. 'But soon as you can, there's a good chap!'

When I had finished, I washed up again and told the steward to hold the next group.

On my way down the alley, a man stepped in front of me.

'Please will you help me?' he pleaded.

He was shabbily dressed and very pale; his features were pinched and he shivered as he spoke.

'I am sorry. I am busy,' I said and attempted to walk on.

'Please, Mr Lasgarn, it's urgent,' he insisted.

How he knew my name I could not guess, but as my mind was filled with the prospective confrontation with Chuffington, I really did not want to be bothered.

Then he clutched the sleeve of my coat.

'It's William,' he said, 'he is very ill.'

'William?' He nodded. 'Your pet?' He nodded again. 'You will have to take him to the surgery,' I said. 'I shall be tied up here all day.'

'I can't,' said the man. 'My wife won't let him out of the house. It's only around the corner. Please come.'

'I've got all these bulls to see to,' I protested. 'It's impossible.'

'Can you come when you've finished?' he persisted.

He really did look desperate and his shivers had turned to shakes.

'Oh, all right,' I agreed, rather irritably. 'Where is it?'

'Fourteen, Goodhope Terrace. Just off Market Street. Doesn't matter how late, but you will come?'

'Yes,' I assured him. 'I will.'

When I got to the Secretary's office, which was a room in the market building, only a young girl clerk was there.

'They've gone to the pen to look at it,' she said. Then tracing the route with her finger on a plan lying on the desk, added. 'Pen fourteen, Row E.'

Slightly flustered, I found Pen fourteen where a small group had gathered around Duncalm Folk Hero. I could see the stockman gesticulating vigorously to a tall military figure in a close-fitting dark green suit and bowler hat.

Wilbert saw me coming and announced my arrival to the tall man.

'The vet, Mr President,' he said sharply.

Mr Chuffington turned towards me and with a wry smile said:

'So you are the chap who wants to throw out my bull!' There was a suggestion of humour in his voice, but only a suggestion.

'I am sorry,' I said. 'But in my opinion it is active ringworm.'

'Ringworm, my arse!' muttered the stockman.

'Pike does not agree,' said Mr Chuffington, 'do you, Pike? He says it is a rub. How sure are you, Mr . . .'

'Lasgarn,' I said. 'Hugh Lasgarn.'

'Standing in for Mr Hacker,' added Wilbert, somewhat tactlessly.

Chuffington raised his bushy eyebrows.

'Mr Hacker is ill,' I explained.

He rubbed his chin thoughtfully. 'How sure are you, Mr Lasgarn?'

'As sure as I can be without a laboratory examination.'

As soon as I had said it, I knew I had complicated the issue and he was quick to take the point.

'So you are not absolutely certain, Mr Lasgarn?'

'Ninety per cent,' I said.

'I had high hopes for this fellow.' He ran his hand across Folk Hero's back. 'This is a very expensive disappointment.'

'Should we have a second opinion?' asked Wilbert.

Chuffington shook his head. 'I will take Mr Lasgarn's word for it – but I would like you to confirm your diagnosis in due course,' he added. 'You can do that?'

'I will take samples and get them tested,' I agreed.

'I think you should,' he said. He raised his bushy eyebrows once again. 'And now we must go and view the judging. Thank you, Mr Lasgarn. No doubt I shall be hearing from you.'

With that he left, followed by Wilbert and several stewards.

'Cost the boss a lot of money if you'm wrong,' said Pike.

Of that I was very much aware and contemplated it off and on for the rest of the day; Duncalm Folk Hero had certainly put a damper on things.

The Supreme Champion went to a bull from Brecon, with Paxton's Donhill Groucho as Reserve; but for me, the euphoria of the occasion was tempered by the upset and I was glad when I was able to get away, just after five o'clock.

I was on the outskirts of Ledingford when I remembered the little man from the market. After saying a few choice words I had to drive a further half-mile before I was able to turn round, and then got snarled up in the rush hour traffic; so that by the time I arrived at Goodhope Terrace, I was not in the best of moods.

I pulled up outside Number Fourteen which, being the same number as the pen of Folk Hero, just added to the annoyance. Goodhope Terrace was indeed a misnomer, for it was a most depressing place, the rain that had filled the night sky adding to the gloom. Three street lamps attempted to give a mite of cheer with little effect, and as I got out of the car, one of them popped and went out. A cold white light shone through the thin curtains in an upstairs room, but for the rest the house was in darkness. Around the dull metal letter box was a handle and I grazed my knuckles on the flap as I rattled it up and down.

Almost immediately I heard hollow footsteps descending the stairway and the hall light came on, illuminating a small window above the door.

The knob twisted and the door opened, grating over the tiles, and there stood the man from the market.

He was in shirt-sleeves and collarless. With the light behind him, I could not see his face; but from his silhouette he looked even more feeble than before.

Then I saw a woman come half-way down the stairs, stop and put her hands to her face.

They both stood and looked at me in silence.

'I've called,' I said; which was a pretty pointless observation, but at least it was something.

Then the man turned to the woman, nodded and brought his hands together in a silent clap, following which he opened his palms towards her in a pushing motion. She bit her thumb hard, then turned and went back up the stairs.

Only then did he thank me for coming and beckoned me to enter.

The hallway was narrow and bare, save for one picture, an old-fashioned piece, with the colours painted in sepia upon the glass. It was of a curly-headed little girl in a taffeta dress and frilly hat, holding a bunch of pansies. In the dim light I could just see her happy, smiling face: a singular ray of joy amidst such drab surroundings.

The man stood back and I made for the door at the end of the passage.

'In here?' I asked, but he put his hand on my shoulder.

'Upstairs,' he said. 'In the bedroom.'

There was just one door open on the landing, leading to the lighted room I had noticed from the street. A damp silence was all about, and I felt uneasy.

The room was sparsely furnished: there was a bed, washstand with a tiled back, and a chest. In the corner near the window stood a cradle and the woman was kneeling and rocking it gently. From inside I could hear a rattling sound and the low moan of distressed breathing. I turned to the man, but he had tears in his eyes and said nothing.

Suddenly I felt inadequate and did not know what to do.

Then the woman reached forward and from inside the cradle gently withdrew a tiny form dressed in blue. Blue bonnet, woolly cardigan and pants covering a napkin.

She stood up, clutching it to her breasts as it fought for breath.

The baby was desperately ill; it was no time to question why they had sent for a vet and not a doctor. If I was to save its life I would have to act quickly and get the child to hospital.

I moved forward to take it from the woman, but she pulled away. As she did so, she turned the little bundle towards me and for the first time I saw its face.

I was shattered, for it was not a child at all.

It was a monkey. A tiny little monkey.

'We lost our baby at birth,' said the man. 'They said my wife could have no more. She went to pieces, so I bought William.' He started to sob, then sniffed deeply and pulled himself together. 'William has been ailing for some time, but she would not let me get anybody in case they took him away.'

I had never been in such a situation. So much for the veterinary syllabus at Glasgow University. So much for training anywhere. What vet can say he was prepared for every eventuality?

'Can I look at it now?' I asked.

I held out my hands and the woman glanced nervously at her husband.

He made a circular movement with his hands and smiled at her; then she passed the tiny creature over to me and I held it – just like a baby – for several minutes.

I placed it on the bed and undid the blue woolly cardigan, beneath which was a vest. Lifting this I listened to its chest with my stethoscope. Despite its distress it watched my every move with its little green eyes. I treated it just like a baby and at one point it curled its tiny fingers around one of mine and gripped quite tightly. It was most disturbing, and as I listened to its heaving chest, my worst fears were confirmed.

Both lungs were waterlogged as a result of an exudative pneumonia; the heart was beginning to weaken and death was inevitable.

I pulled down the tiny vest and tucked it in; then buttoned up the blue woolly cardigan and gave William back to the woman.

'No hope,' said the man.

'I am sorry,' I said.

'We don't want him to suffer,' said the man. 'Will you put him to sleep?'

I suddenly felt a great hollowness inside of me and I couldn't speak. I looked at the woman cuddling her child substitute and tried to pull myself together. Everything started to close in upon me; the front bedroom at Number Fourteen, Goodhope Terrace became a contracting box.

I could not do it – could not kill the little creature. It was immoral. William was more than just an animal.

I began searching for excuses – maybe I was being precipitous – penicillin could help, and if it did not, William would die naturally. But that could be days. Days of suffering and agony. Putting him to sleep was the most humane thing to do.

'The incentive to cure disease and ease suffering and the courage to take life when pain is beyond control . . .'

My personal veterinary philosophy was being put to the test.

'She does understand?' I asked eventually.

He did not answer, but sat on the bed beside his wife. She turned to him and he took her face gently in both hands and looked deeply into her tear-filled eyes. I saw his lips moving slowly and deliberately and only then did I realize the other great tragedy.

For she was mute, both deaf and dumb.

How long they sat I do not know, for it was one of those gaps in time that have no dimension.

She held William whilst I gave the injection and her husband had his arm around her shoulders. The little creature clung to her all the way, its breathing first rapid, then gentle – then it was all so peaceful – and over.

I stayed until I was absolutely sure.

Then I left them sitting together on the bed and let myself out.

And that is the very special reason why I shall never forget my first Hereford Bull Sale.

10

'Got it playing cricket,' said the Reverend Mr Simms as he
tugged the reluctant 'sportsman' into the surgery. 'A real
shiner.'

Elijah, his Pembrokeshire Corgi, looked up, one eye
closed and swollen.

'Cricket is a game for Gentlemen and Players,' I said.
'Where does Elijah fit in?'

'Best long-stop in these parts,' he continued, lifting the
squat little fellow onto the table. 'Only a soft ball, you
understand; plays all day if the boys want to and rarely
lets one pass – but he was not paying attention on this
occasion and the poor chap caught one in the eye.'

I gently examined Elijah's injury.

'Odd thing was,' explained the vicar, 'it improved by
itself the following day, then about four days ago it swelled
up again. I got quite worried because Mr Pont, the Churchwarden, told me Corgis were prone to eye ulcers. Do you
think Elijah's got one?'

It was true that Corgis are one of the breeds that are
susceptible to peculiar eye reactions that can sometimes
lead to corneal erosion, but often, after a blow, infection
can enter and I suspected that this had happened to Elijah.

I instilled a few drops of a fluorescing agent into the eye
to show up any ulceration. Elijah submitted to the performance well, for unco-operative patients who insist on closing
their eyelids can make things very difficult.

Whilst I was conducting my examination, the vicar was
saying how busy he was and that he had to rush off
afterwards to conduct a party of historians around the
church.

'I hope they do not want to go up the tower,' he said, as

I switched off my ophthalmoscope. 'I have not got Elijah's energy, more is the pity.'

I prescribed some antibiotic drops for Elijah, which would take care of the trouble, and explained the course of treatment.

'Wouldn't mind going up the tower myself sometime,' I said, as they prepared to leave. 'It would be nice to have an owl's eye view of Welbury.'

'Certainly, my boy,' he said willingly. 'Any time. Just pick up the key from the vicarage, it is truly a remarkable sight . . . but you mean "a bird's eye view".'

'No,' I said. ' "Owl's eye".'

He smiled, said, 'Of course,' then departed with Elijah, a slightly bemused expression upon his face.

The afternoon I decided to make my ascent was warm and clear.

'Good day for it,' said the vicar, when I called to collect the ancient, well-worn key. 'You will be able to see for miles.'

Though old and despite a little jiggling, when I finally managed to fit the iron piece into the lock of the small oak door at the foot of the tower, the bolt snapped back easily.

Accompanied by an Alfred Hitchcock-type groan, the hinges turned and I stepped inside the great stone edifice.

The staircase was spiral and clockwise, the steps worn and narrow, and the only illumination a dusty shaft of sunlight sneaking through a narrow single trefoiled window. In the cool, damp air I trod the steps winding my way upwards, and though but only yards away from home and surgery, I felt I was being drawn backwards in time.

The tower, built in the early fourteenth century, was reputed to have been a place of refuge, and as I climbed amid the ever deepening gloom, I sensed the shuffling of feet other than my own, the nervous chatter of voices, the whimpering of children as the souls of Welbury gathered for protection within the mighty walls.

After some forty steps and several spirals, I came to a door that led to the bellringer's room. There, like the fluffy tails of monsters roosting up above, hung the ropes, tasselled and still. Odd and so detached they appeared, such unlikely triggers of the fulsome sound.

Upwards I toiled to the clock room, where stood the ironframed workings, the guts of the timepiece that graced the south face. 'One Day Telleth Another and One Night Certifieth Another,' read the inscription. The weights and wheels, all greased and solid, slowly clicked the seconds by, measuring the span of all below in equal parts.

Then onward to the bells.

There were six in all and 'up'. The vicar had warned me that in such a position they were finely balanced and had advised me not to touch anything. I stood there on the platform in the uncanny silence, scarcely breathing lest the bells should drop at my presence.

What a mighty mass of iron, smelted and cast by men like my forebears in Abergranog: mining and furnacing the earth's minerals; sweating and toiling to mould and hang such things for the Glory of God.

They rung roughly in the key of E. The tenor, a massive cast of 19cwt, was inscribed, 'Be it known to all men that John Martin of Wossister made me – All men that hear my roaring sound, Repent before ye be in ground.'

Roaring maybe, but inanimate and impotent without the hand of man, either in its birth or motion; yet it was a fearsome thing and as I read the words, it was as if they had been spoken. For in their song, all six sounded words to the people in days gone by – the village newspaper or the radio broadcast. The Churchwarden's book records that the bells of Welbury celebrated almost every event 'in the neighbourhood of history'.

These included Oak Apple Day, which may have been introduced to emphasize the relationship between the Hanoverians and the Jacobites; Powder Plot, better known as Guy Fawkes Day; the Battle of the Boyne in 1690, and the defeat of the Young Pretender in 1745. They were rung whenever an English monarch returned in safety from abroad, and also to stress the solidarity of the Allied cause;

for Marlborough's victories and for 'peace between France and ye Emperor'.

For every celebration the ringers received 5s and, on very special occasions, ale.

The bells rang a muffled peal on Holy Innocents Day; the tenor bell was tolled at a funeral as the mourners approached; there was also a toll within twelve hours of a death, regulated by the age of the dead person.

In the eighteenth century, the curfew was rung at eight o'clock every night.

Truly it was the ancient version of the news room.

There were 120 steps in all, and I counted every one.

Finally I pushed on another small door, similar to that at the foot of the tower, and fresh, clean air and sunshine cascaded about me. I felt like a mole breaking through the earthy crust; but moles are blind and more is the pity, for the view that met my gaze, as I straightened my stooping body, was breathtaking.

Being closeted in the darkness of the staircase and breaking my ascent at the various stages, I had not been aware of the height to which I was climbing. And though the whole structure appeared quite massive from the ground, the parapet was narrow and a feeling of vertigo welled up inside me when first I looked down upon the village.

How neat it was and peaceful: from the gravestones right below, along the narrow lane to the square, the houses, shops and pubs, my own house and surgery, all just like a child's toys.

One felt able to reach out and pick up the buildings, turn them about, put the few cars in a more orderly fashion or spread the bunch of cows in Basset's field, to order. How cheeky it would be to move the cottage of Miss Moffat, a staunch teetotaller, next door to the Red Lion; or Ken Bates' pigs behind Sheena's Hairdressing Salon. What on earth would she say?' I smiled when I remembered the fuss there had been when a furniture business moved in to the adjoining shop. The windows ran more or less together and the lettering, looking as if it was continuous, read:

Ladies' Hairdresser, Perms and Rinses . . . Stripping and Remodelling, Sliding Drawers A Speciality

Mr Wedgewood's car was parked outside, waiting patiently for his wife who was having her weekly 'do'.

Mr Wedgewood, the most expensive consultation I ever gave.

He had come to live in Welbury from Wolverhampton where he had an engineering business and, hoping to sell up and retire in a few years, had bought Well Cottage. I first met him when he arrived at surgery with a Yellow Labrador called Skipper.

'Can you give me something that will stop him getting agitated and violently sick in the car?' he asked, explaining that both he and his wife travelled daily to their factory and could not leave Skipper behind. 'If we do, he howls incessantly and tears the place up,' he said in despair. 'We have tried everything . . . pills, potions, hung chains from the car, changed his diet, rubbed half an onion on the windscreen, even played "Doggy" music, to no avail. Driving me mad, he is!' he exclaimed. 'The wife will not stay behind and look after the menace; he cannot be left alone and it is hell driving with him. What on earth can I do?'

I gave Skipper a thorough examination. He was a big, friendly chap and did not seem the sort to throw a tantrum; following Mr Wedgewood's description of the previous treatment, I was at a loss to know what to prescribe.

'Got a proper set-up for him in the back of the car. Railed off and very comfortable,' said Mr Wedgewood, with a sigh.

'What sort of car is it?' I enquired.

He mentioned a popular continental model.

'Good car,' I said, 'though I was never very keen on rear engines.'

I paused as the thought struck me: Mr Wedgewood's facial expression anticipated my next comment. 'Try another car,' I suggested, 'perhaps Skipper doesn't like rear engines either!'

When next we met, Mr Wedgewood was sitting in a luxurious British limousine with a happy Skipper reclining in the back like a company director.

'It worked?' I enquired hesitantly.

'Eventually,' he replied. 'Tested fifteen different cars. The ones he liked, she didn't,' he nodded to the passenger seat, 'and the ones she liked, he didn't!' he jerked his thumb over his shoulder towards Skipper, who wagged his tail approvingly. 'This was the only one. Beats me,' he added, shaking his head gravely, 'which are the most expensive, dogs or women!'

'I heard that!' said his wife.

'Woof!' barked Skipper.

'Best to Buy British!' I called and as they drove away I felt my diagnosis had not only helped their problem, but also done a bit for the home market as well.

But distance lends enchantment and Mr Wedgewood's car was just a dinky toy below. His wife emerged from Sheena's redfaced, with her hair piled up on top; I heard Skipper bark his approval or otherwise and they glided off up the street.

From the tower, the gardens of the village showed up well: Welbury was a self-sufficient little place when it came to fruit and veg. I could see Mr White putting something on his beans with a watering can – best beans in the village and never used any additives . . . or so he said!

And there was Turk, coming from the butcher's yard with a bone . . . he struggled with his possession through a hole in the fence and into the adjoining market garden, running through the potato rows and skirting the greenhouse; he dropped down to the stream, jumped it and slipped through the hedge at the back of the Police House where he lived. Still at it, I mused, despite the trouble.

Turk was one of two dogs belonging to PC Packham; he was a rather nondescript but amiable mongrel, whereas his kennel companion, Ben, was a tough liver and white

Springer. They were great pals and loved nothing more than a romp over the fields under Bob Packham's watchful supervision. So when Turk turned up with a swollen ear and a gaping wound below it, I was surprised to learn that Ben had been the culprit.

It was a nasty wound and I had to use sedation before I could suture; it took six stitches and, as I worked away, Bob explained what had happened.

'If both dogs are free in the garden, they have been known to take off for a bit of a run and I'm the last person to allow them loose in the countryside so I always fasten one or t'other up on a long lead.

'Now if Turk isn't tied, he often pops up to the butcher for some bones. First he brings one for Ben, then goes back and gets one for himself.'

'A very generous gesture,' I agreed.

'It was his generosity that got him into trouble,' Bob continued.

It transpired that Turk happily delivered the first bone, but had a bit of a nose-about on his second trip and was some time returning. When he did, he unwittingly dropped his own bone within reach of Ben, who had already demolished most of his and buried the rest.

Ben, still feeling a little peckish, decided to help himself to Turk's bone and that was how the fight started.

Fortunately, the wound healed well, but it was a reminder of how easily companionship can be forgotten and basic instincts take over.

'I hope you've had a word with Ben,' I said, as they left the surgery.

'They have both been cautioned,' came the stern reply.

Yet from what I could see from my lofty vantage point, Turk, for one, had not taken it too seriously.

* * *

Welbury village sits rather like a hub in the centre of a cartwheel with five roads radiating at intervals from it; yet surprisingly enough, it is on the road to nowhere. This is because the major routes from England into Wales run both north and south of the village, carrying most of the traffic directly past, and one has to make a detour to come our way.

Not so in days gone by, when Welbury was the centre of commerce and interest in the area; to the extent that it had turnpikes on the roads to collect tolls and the rules were strictly kept: in 1840 a man who tried to smuggle a bag of beans through the Welbury Lane turnpike gate was fined £15 and the loss of his horse by local magistrates – a harsh levy, giving us little grounds for complaint when modern custom officers spot our excess 'duty free'.

The Welbury of today is without the bustle of old, for though there is an annual carnival, in past times it held many fairs and celebrated with fervour every event of national importance.

Like all country fairs, they were great occasions for the showing of livestock and not without the element of keen competition and even some subterfuge; indeed there is recorded the case of one man who was summoned for giving his cattle juniper, rue and mednip to improve their appearance.

Competition raged not only amongst the locals, but between villages for the best fair, and Welbury was scathingly reported when it started to decline in popularity as mostly consisting of 'but one small cow, a calf and five small steers and Welsh runts and no price asked'.

The present carnival centres on the Castle Green where for many years open air dinners were held to celebrate great occasions, such as the accession and marriage of Queen Victoria, royal births and virtually any excuse for jubilation when much beef, bread and cider were consumed.

Food then was rich and wholesome and fads and fancies not respected; as my eye wandered from the Castle Green, shaded by the great oaks, I caught sight of Doris Perciman, scurrying across the square with a basket of shopping, and wondered how she might have fared in those times.

Doris lived at Number One, Bye Street, but it was her

sister Emily who had come to my surgery shortly after I arrived in Welbury.

She placed a large wicker basket on the table, opened the grille and carefully slid out a lace cushion on which reclined a thin grey cat.

'You see,' said Emily, folding her arms, 'she has no life in her at all. All day she just lies on her cushion and only rarely ventures outside, and ours is such a lovely garden.'

She was right about the garden in which the two sisters worked diligently throughout the year; but as she spoke, the little cat just stared disinterestedly ahead, as if bored by the whole affair.

I lifted her gently from the cushion; she was certainly lifeless and hung limply in my arms.

'Any signs of illness?' I enquired. 'Any coughs, sneezes or running eyes?' Emily shook her head. 'What are you feeding her on?' I asked.

Emily Perciman stroked the grey fur and sighed.

'I think that could be the trouble,' she said. 'You see, Willow is not my cat, she belongs to my sister and she is a vegetarian.'

I guessed what was coming next.

'She feeds Willow on the same food that she eats herself, nut cutlets, lentil roasts and the like. She insists that meat is poison and that Willow is far better without it; but I am sure that Doris is wrong.'

'Your sister certainly is,' I confirmed, explaining to Emily that cats have very special dietary needs, for being true carnivores they must have certain amino-acids in their food that are only found in animal protein. Dogs can be vegetarians, but cats cannot.

'She gives her vegetables,' said Emily, 'I suppose that helps.'

'Not really,' I told her. 'Cats cannot cope with high fibre diets. Of course, an all-meat diet can give problems too, so balance is the answer. The tinned foods available are very well formulated and should satisfy Willow's needs.'

'Will you ring my sister and explain?' she asked. 'She might listen to you.'

So ring Doris Perciman I did. She was surprisingly affable and accepted my advice.

'I will pick up some tinned food on my way home,' said Emily, looking much relieved.

'Change the diet gradually,' I advised, 'and you should have a much happier cat in a short while.'

Emily popped Willow back into her basket. 'I will take charge of her from now on,' she said, then added with a smile. 'I think I shall tell my sister to get a rabbit.'

Which she duly did and, looking down at the garden of Number One, Bye Street, I could see the hutch even now, at the back of the cherry tree.

My village practice included many furry pets and one of the first I encountered in Welbury presented a most unusual situation.

It was late one evening when the man turned up, most frightening in his appearance; a walking mountain if ever I saw one, who blocked out the daylight as he stood in my doorway, cradling in his treetrunk arms what appeared to be a box shrouded with a white sheet.

With some difficulty he negotiated the entrance and set his charge down upon the table with exceptional gentleness; then he carefully removed the sheet to reveal a bright wire cage. At first it appeared empty until I detected a slight movement amongst the wood shavings on its floor and up popped the head of a tiny gerbil.

As are all gerbils, it was extremely curious and soon emerged to stand erect upon its long hind legs, studying the surroundings intently with large brown eyes.

When I remarked on the similarity of its stance to a tiny kangaroo, the man put a massive hand upon my shoulder that weighed like a ton.

'I call him Barton,' he said, looking at me most oddly, as if I was meant to understand the reason why.

'What is the problem?' I asked, easing from beneath his hold.

'They said he wouldn't bite,' he explained. 'So last night I tried to catch him. It took me a long time but I got him in

165

the end and held him in my hand, properly like I was told. I know their tails will break off if you hold them by the end, so I held him right down low. He sat there for a few minutes and I was ever so pleased, he seemed to have taken to me – and I had to have that.'

He looked down at me in a manner which, though not menacing, was again compelling me to understand.

I sensed there was something odd about the whole affair and felt a trifle uneasy; this massive man and a tiny gerbil, it was incongruous to say the least.

'He was so happy,' he continued, his eyes shifting to the tiny creature, 'sitting there in my hand.' Then the man's great frame shuddered and he turned to face me again, but with tears streaming down his face. 'He just fell over on his side,' he sobbed. 'Fell over, lifeless – but I never touched him . . . never!' His great hand fell upon my shoulder once again, demanding my sympathy. 'I thought Barton was going to die, you understand. Die!'

'Has he done it before?' I asked, trying to keep things calm.

He eyed me curiously, then nodded slowly and the tears welled up in his eyes for the second time.

'When it happened, what did you do?' I asked him, gently.

'Put him back in his cage.' He moved his great hands expressively.

'Then what?'

'In a few minutes he seemed to get better – but I've been afraid to touch him ever since – but I never hurt him . . . !'

'I'm sure you didn't,' I said, realizing that he was emotionally very upset. 'I suspect it was a fit,' I explained, 'and what has happened is not uncommon in gerbils.'

His great head lowered close to mine, eager for more information.

'Undue stress can produce an apparent fit that may last for several minutes,' I continued. 'It is a defence mechanism, shamming to deceive the opponent.'

At that remark, my Man-Mountain client stood back a

pace; then, with the footwork of a dancer, he shadow-boxed around the surgery, grunting loudly at each thrust. After some time he stopped, closed his eyes and stood silently.

Eventually he recovered and assumed relative normality again.

'So I didn't hurt him?' he said.

'No,' I agreed, thankful that he had composed himself; for had he got further disturbed, he could have been more trouble than a dozen German Shepherds. 'But here is a tip for the future,' I said, taking a small jam jar from the cupboard. 'This is a good method for any small creatures like gerbils, hamsters or mice.' Then, cautiously taking the top off the cage, I gently introduced the jar and coaxed Barton into it. Then I was able to remove him without any fuss and gently restrain him by the base of the tail in my cupped hand.

'This cuts out excess stress when catching, which is maybe why you had the trouble,' I explained, 'with this method you should avoid the fits, especially as he gets used to you.'

I placed the gerbil into the waiting hands and he sat there quite happily, twitching his whiskers.

'You were only shamming, Barton,' the man cooed. 'Just like old times. I know you and your tricks, you crafty beggar, you . . .'

We replaced the gerbil in his cage, he asked if he could have the jam pot, then, after thanking me, he lumbered off down the drive.

It had been an odd consultation and it was some time before I knew what it had been all about.

His name was Gordon Thanet and he lived with his widowed mother; his weight was twenty stones and he was in the fight game. Gordon was very successful taking part in heavy-weight bouts and contests throughout the Midlands, until tragedy struck.

In a fight in Wolverhampton, he was matched against an up-and-coming young heavy-weight several years his junior. It was firmly expected that Gordon would lose, for although good in his day, he was beginning to fade and the bout had more or less been set up to show off the young contender.

The boy was good, of that there was no doubt – but he knew it and instead of confining his efforts to the physical contest, started verbal tactics, mouthing insults as he danced around the old campaigner.

The more he taunted, the more incensed Gordon became, not being used to such ploys. His temper led to rage, until many said he seemed like a man possessed, for in the tenth round he crashed through his opponent's guard with a violent blow that floored him instantaneously – and the boy went into a coma and never recovered.

Gordon Thanet gave up boxing, and though completely exonerated, became very depressed. He rarely went from the house and turned his attention to very delicate things, such as flowers and watercolour painting, as if trying to escape from the brutality and coarseness of his previous occupation. It was suggested he get a pet, and that was when he bought Barton, named after his opponent on that terrible night.

Bad luck, fate or what you will, the gerbil died within six months, why I never knew. And Gordon got so depressed he had to be taken into care.

An odd tale, but then truth is often stranger than fiction, even in Welbury village.

There was Charlie Bales' horse, Davo, who could kick the eye out of a needle . . . but give him a Polo Mint to suck and in ten seconds flat you could do anything at all with the cantankerous old nag.

Mrs Edwardson's German Shepherd, Max, who was both deaf and practically blind, yet only she and I knew that; for she kept The Link, one of the two pubs in the village, all by herself and Max was her guard dog. At closing time he would come and sit on the steps behind the bar and growl menacingly, which was quite enough to dissuade any would-be late drinkers.

There was Ada Cannock at Lilac Cottage and her black tom Sidney for whom she had installed a quite expensive

168

cat flap, which Sidney refused to use . . . that was until I went to give him a shot for 'flu.

He was snoozing in his chair when I entered the room, so I was able to sneak up to him and give him his jab in the backside; the action took Sidney so completely by surprise that he gave a delayed almighty howl and shot straight through the virgin cat flap like a rocket – and from that day, he has used it ever since!

I stood on the parapet and surveyed my domain. What a mix of pets and people, and, as the village vet, how much I knew about them all.

11

Whilst the owl's eye view of Welbury village would have varied in the short term in intimate detail, the general picture of the surrounding countryside had been relatively slow to change, but change it had.

The improvement in road structure had meant an increase in traffic movement, made obvious by the speed and noise of vehicles as they darted from England into Wales. Between the arteries of communication, farm and field sizes had altered, in the main growing larger by virtue of hedgerow removal and woodland clearance. The pattern of cultivation over the years had become smoother and more uniform, aided by sophisticated machinery that was lessening the toil and improving the standard of husbandry in a very dramatic fashion.

Yields had increased in every way with more tonnage of corn and potatoes to the acre, more apples on the trees and hops on the vine, and in the arable sector that was regarded as very acceptable efficiency; but when it came to livestock development it was different, and matters of ethics and morality entered into the reasoning in a manner that often challenged the justification of superproduction.

As my eye followed the wooded skyline to the west, I picked up the pasture land of Wormcastle where Reg and Harry Payne farmed, still in traditional fashion.

'Yer got to be self-supportin',' Reg would say. 'Put back what yer takes. Mustn't force nature, you see. Lead 'er, not force 'er. Just like they nice young fillies I expect you gets yer 'ands on, Hugh! Just like they – eh, 'Arry?'

That of course was in my bachelor days and Harry, his brother, would widen his face by a good two inches either side, raise his rosy cheeks like little cider apples, part his lips to show an assortment of nutbrown teeth and raise his shoulders without making a sound. The perfect mime for a chortle, cackle or laugh, but never a sound.

What a grand pair they were and how charitable they had been to me during my early days in practice; well did I remember my first solo caesarian on a heifer at Wormcastle, which died unexpectedly three days later.

'You can't win 'em all,' Harry had said, in a sincere attempt to console me; yet he and Reg were the ones who had really suffered the loss. Nature's gentlemen they were and would no doubt go on farming in the style of their forefathers with sheep, corn, hops, apples and Herefords. Even though the afternoon sun was bright in that direction, I could pick out the rich red coats of the pedigrees standing out against the lush green sward; some half-dozen were lying in the shade of a pair of giant oaks, contented and unrestrained.

Yet just over the hill, not half a mile away, lay Barrington, where progress in livestock husbandry had created a very different scene.

It was Bob Hacker who first got the approach from Ben Hallett, the manager of the new pig unit that was to be established there.

'It will be good business for us, Hugh,' said Bob, when he rang one morning with the news, 'and as it's in your area, I suggested you would call and see him. The buildings will be completed this week and he should be stocking up before the end of the month.'

'I hear it is going to be pretty intensive,' I commented. 'Already raised a few hackles round and about.'

'It's got to be, Hugh,' said Bob. 'It's how things are going these days. Anyway as long as it's done properly, and it will be; there's no shortage of cash.'

'Who is behind it?' I asked.

'Didn't you know?' exclaimed Bob. 'It's your mate, Paxton!'

'Never mentioned a thing to me,' I said.

'Close old beggar when it comes to business,' Bob

171

replied. 'Anyway, call in and see the manager chap, I expect he can fill you in more on the details.'

Paxton of Donhill had featured prominently in my veterinary career, from my very early days in Ledingford.

To me the old tyrant epitomized all that was truculent in veterinary clients: wealthy, demanding, short of temper and frighteningly intolerant; yet over the years, after surviving many confrontations and crises with him, surprisingly enough I had come to like, even respect him and felt in his own way that he reciprocated.

Our friendship was what one might refer to in medical terms as 'sub-clinical' – present, but not very obvious.

It had developed through chance when I stuck my neck out in my first, tentative weeks in practice and operated upon his champion bull, Warrior. The procedure was to remove surgically some persistent corns from between the massive animal's toes, under general anaesthetic; it was a new technique and put my reputation very firmly on the line, as well as my sanity at the time. But it was a success, and from that day forward our blustery relationship had developed, enhanced by a little asthmatic boy called Billy Bent whose budgerigar had died. Paxton had introduced Billy to his fish collection, a fantasy of colour and movement which he had installed at his great house.

Billy, who had always wanted to be a 'bird vet', asked Paxton if he could become a 'fish vet' instead, and the old man had said he would see to it and took the little orphan lad under his wing. Billy had responded marvellously to Paxton's help and was now well on the way towards his ambition.

Through such involvement, although I was not exactly his bosom pal – no one could ever have been that – he had confided in me on several occasions and told me a lot about his past; so I was mystified and even a trifle hurt that he should embark upon such a revolutionary livestock enterprise without so much as a word to me.

I had firmly intended to call at Barrington on several occasions, but each time I was thwarted by emergencies.

However, as I had been driving by on other calls, I had taken note how development was progressing.

The unit was not readily visible from the road, being built on a plateau mechanically excavated from the side of the hill, so that just the roof apex of each building could be seen; one could glimpse three sections, but there was little hint as to size, for the whole construction was so carefully blended into the background that it in no way upset the landscape, or perhaps it was meant to be out of sight. However, before I did have a closer inspection and meet the manager, I had occasion to visit Donhill.

I did not see Paxton on every visit, unlike the early days when he was always breathing down my neck. I dealt mostly with Mason, the head stockman; but as it happened both of them were in the yard when I arrived to see if some heifers were in-calf.

'I want these pregnancies accurate,' Paxton growled at me as I got out of the car. No 'Good morning' or 'How are you?' – he was on form, all right.

'They will be,' I said. 'Mornin' Dan,' acknowledging Mason, then without so much as a glance at Paxton I went round to the boot of the car and prepared my gear.

'How many are they?' I enquired, counting the disposable plastic gloves.

'Quite a few,' Dan Mason replied.

'Quite a few!' raged Paxton. 'What the hell does that mean?'

"Bout seventeen,' said Mason, again with typical Herefordian vagueness, yet within the limits of local accuracy.

By now I was well versed in such estimations and fully aware that in farming parlance 'a few' was up to three; 'a fair few' up to seven; 'quite a few' could be fifteen to twenty, and 'a good few' from twenty upwards.

But Paxton, despite being longer domiciled in the county than myself, still had not grasped such parochial terminology.

'About! About! Why about, man?' he railed.

"Cos we didn't bring 'em all up at once,' explained Mason in a rather bored tone. 'There's thirty-four down

there, reckon we brought up about 'alf . . . an' that . . .'
he nodded, as if to emphasize his reasoning, '. . . is about
seventeen.'

I let the two banter away as to why there was not
enough room to collect the whole bunch, and donned my
boots and apron.

'My God!' Paxton finally slammed his cane into the
ground. 'You can't manage with that? What do you expect
me to do . . . build another cattle unit?'

'Or a pig unit,' I remarked.

He spun round.

'What d'ye mean?' He glared at me intently.

'I heard you had an interest in Barrington – kept it a bit
quiet, didn't you?'

He grunted and turned slightly. 'I've only got a financial
interest. I've nothing to do with the running of it; but I did
tell the manager to get in touch with your firm.'

'He has,' I said. 'Just thought it a bit odd you not
mentioning it.'

'Slipped my mind,' he said irritably.

Now I knew from experience that nothing, absolutely
nothing ever slipped Paxton's mind – there was more to
this than met the eye.

'Didn't you think I knew enough about pigs?' I
challenged.

'Mason, go and get the cattle sorted.' Paxton waved his
cane and Mason dutifully left.

'Did you want someone else to do the work?' I persisted.

I expected him to say 'no' immediately; but he did not,
which rather took me by surprise.

'I did not think you would want it,' he said, looking me
hard in the face.

'Of course we would want it!' I exclaimed. 'We are
always looking for expansion.'

'"We",' said Paxton, 'I said "you". I did not think you
would want it. It is a new system, all undercover . . .
automatic feed . . . restricted light and movement . . .
sows in stalls and weaning at five days. I did not think you
would approve.'

174

His facial expression softened and he almost smiled in a mildly fatherly manner.

'They call it "Factory Farming",' he said.

What an enigma that old man was. One minute bawling out half the world and kicking it in the rump, trampling on anyone he felt was in his way; yet deep down having consideration for my feelings about rearing pigs.

Factory farming. My mind ran back to Lydia Belmont and her outburst at the WI: 'Belsen, how can you condone it?' she had all but screamed.

But she was an emotional and rather way-out young woman; her views were in many respects predictable. Yet Paxton, a hard-headed businessman, even he had reservations; clouded maybe by his arrogant attitude, but they were there – I could sense them.

'You once said to me you liked working in the Borders because it was as close to nature as farming could get and still be economical.' Paxton eyed me questioningly.

True, I had said that, and meant it. To me Herefordshire and the Welsh Marches were a gentle blend of animal husbandry and environment; a combination that seemed so right, and although stocking rates had increased, there was still a freedom that both animals and people were privileged to share; a freedom that was lacking in many other places. But with all he had: 'Do you really need it?' I asked him.

Suddenly Paxton was back to his old ebullient self. 'As a commercial enterprise it is a sound investment,' he retorted, 'the projected figures are good, and if a succession of this type of enterprise can be set up, it is an excellent proposition.' Then he looked away from me and added, 'Anyway, if I don't do it, someone else will.'

'And if I don't do the work – likewise!' I said.

He looked back at me, frowned, then said, 'Yes!'

'We don't have anything like it in the practice, so I admit I have no first-hand knowledge of the system, but it is becoming established and, as a profession, we have to be involved; that doesn't mean to say one has to condone it in principle.'

'You eat pork, don't you?' he snapped.

Then he was off across the yard, tapping his cane as he went and shunning any further involvement in the ethics of animal welfare.

One could say: 'There is no answer to that.'

Yet I felt there must be.

It was a dull mist-laden afternoon when I called at Barrington; low grey cloud hung over the woodland ridge behind the site, threatening to drift even further down the slopes in a sinister attempt to squeeze out the remaining daylight.

Across the newly laid driveway stood two high boarded gates, which, together with the equally high continuous larchlap panel, fencing prevented any view of the interior.

The atmosphere that pervaded the construction was sombre and silent, accentuated by the murky weather, and the description of 'unit' seemed unsettlingly apt; whereas farms, pastures or even a whitewashed sty had gentle, rural tones, the term 'pig units' sounded devoid of all feeling.

And that was what the large white board on the right hand gate proclaimed:

BARRINGTON PIG UNITS
NO UNAUTHORIZED PERSON BEYOND THIS POINT
RING BELL FOR ATTENTION

However, there was no sign of bell or button, and finding the doors unlatched, I pushed them ajar and entered.

It was an eerie experience, for as yet the premises were unoccupied and all was still and noiseless. There were three buildings, as I had guessed from my glimpse of the upper structure from the road; they ran endlessly in parallel back into the plot. Wooden walled in construction, the felted roofs carried large chimney ventilators at intervals, protruding through each apex. The windows were plentiful but of opaque glass reinforced with wire netting. The flooring all about was new white concrete, ridged to give grip and drained in several directions.

'UNIT ONE', said the sign on the first building, and I went inside.

The first section was the food storage and preparation room with large pipes running from a great mixer into metal bins on wheels, with weight gauges attached. In one corner was a small partitioned area with a window through which I spied a desk, wall charts and a great panel of switches like the control room of a power station – a far cry from Reg and Harry Payne's 'meal and root house', where mangels and swedes were chopped and oats and barley caringly mixed by hand. It was a unit all right: a technological breeding and fattening factory, where the inmates would never know the sun on their backs.

The next door was aluminium and stuck on its runners, despite its newness; but when it did yield it revealed what was probably the most contentious part of the whole system – the sow stalls.

Four rows, one running down each wall and two in the centre; each railed in tubular steel from its neighbour, just wide enough and long enough for one sow. In the front of each was a concrete trough with a water spout, activated by pressure of snout on nozzle. The floor again was of ridged white concrete, sloping backwards to a continuous drainage channel, and overhead ran banks of neon lights.

Halfway down and built into the roof was a giant extractor fan which was in action, despite the building being empty. It functioned with a deep, friendly hum – the only consoling feature in the whole sinister design.

I lost count at 200 spaces, for 200 sows. I could not imagine such a number in one group – or perhaps I did not want to.

'Yes sir! What can I do for you?'

The sharp, rather hostile enquiry came from behind and I turned to find a red-faced man with glasses standing in the doorway.

In his fifties, I guessed, his unruly hair topped by a cloth cap; for the rest he was attired in a boiler suit and spotless white wellington boots – certainly not dressed to match.

'Just having a look,' I said, caught slightly off guard.

'I can see that,' he said irritably. 'And who might you be?'

'Hugh Lasgarn. I've been asked to do the work here.'

'Work!'

'Veterinary work. Hacker and Lasgarn from Ledingford, I live in Welbury, just over the hill.'

He nodded, relaxing his rather threatening manner.

'Ben Hallett,' he announced, holding out a hand. 'Didn't know you were coming. Thought you were a "snooper" – we've had a few of them already.'

'I would have rung the bell, but I couldn't find it,' I explained.

'There isn't one yet,' he said, 'but that is all there is to fix.'

'How many will it take?' I asked, stepping over towards the stalls.

'Two hundred and twenty,' he replied.

'And how long will they be in here?'

'How long?' he retorted. 'What do you mean?'

'Confined in these stalls.'

'Apart from farrowing – all the time. Why?'

'For life,' I said.

'Christ! Don't tell me I've got a bloody squeamish vet to deal with!' Ben Hallett exploded.

'No,' I countered, slowly but deliberately. 'But I haven't had anything to do with this type of system before and the principle takes some initial understanding.'

'Sorry,' said Ben. 'But I have said this piece until I am blue in the face: if the public want pork and bacon on their plates at a reasonable price – and they do! – then it has got to be produced in a fast, efficient manner to a standard quality. This is the system that will do it.'

'What about the pigs – their welfare?' I questioned.

'What's wrong with it?' His mood was bordering again upon the aggressive. 'They are housed, fed regularly, kept healthy and are doing the job they were made for – breeding. What they have to give up is freedom – the freedom of wallowing in cold mud, getting chilled, lamed, starved and left to take their own chance. Anyways, those that come in here have never known anything different – put them in the care of Mother Nature and they will die.'

'But they can't even turn round,' I said. 'Like battery hens.'

Ben Hallett sighed wearily. 'If it were not for man producing them, hens or pigs, they wouldn't be here at all; they would never even know what life was. At least they experience the basic sensations of "being"; they know eating, smelling, seeing and feeling – even though it is like bloody prison! Tell me, Mr Lasgarn, is it better to be born a battery hen or never be born at all?'

His reasoning was not without some logic and I took his point.

'But even you call it a prison,' I argued. 'Are you completely happy with it?'

'Happy?' Ben Hallett shook his head and smiled wistfully, then leaned back against the doorpost. 'You was never in the War, Mr Lasgarn, was you?' I shook my head. 'No, too young you would be,' he continued, gazing beyond me, his eyes lost in reminiscence.

'Come off the *George the Fifth* at Casablanca, slept under me gas cape the first few nights, then rode me arse off across North Africa – despatch rider, I was. Through the desert with Monty, then up into Italy. Monte Casino, saw me pals blown up like confetti in the wind.

'Over the Alps into the Fatherland – and I was at Belsen.' Then he took a deep breath and paused.

In that last sentence, though he had not said it, he had qualified his outlook and put his personal humanitarianism into perspective; though what he told me next would equally have done so, for he shook his head and then in a quiet voice said:

'Survived it all, the terror and the carnage. Then come home to find my wife terminally ill, and a month after she died, my only boy was killed – riding a bloody motor bike.'

I did not know what to say and for some time we stood in silence, a silence emphasized by the starkness of our surroundings. Ben Hallett's gaze shortened and he looked directly at me again.

179

'Mr Lasgarn,' he continued. 'I have seen some sights that no man should see and I have known more loss and desperation than most. I started working with pigs because it was the only job I could get at the time. Shovelling pig shit – that was my reward for helping to save my Country.

'But I stuck it and went up in the ranks until I was manager of Swaby's in Yorkshire; a thousand sows we had then and it was there that I helped to develop this system and make it as efficient and as humane as I could.' He rearranged his cap on his head, then folded his arms tightly. 'No, of course I am not happy with it,' he admitted; then his face softened into a craggy smile. 'But I'll tell you, Mr Lasgarn, there's many a time in my life when I would gladly have swapped my lot for grub, a place to lie down and no responsibility. You can't have it all ways, Mr Lasgarn – none of us can.' He clapped his hands together and stood away from the wall. 'Now then,' he said in a cheery fashion, 'if you like and you can stomach it, I'll give you a tour of the rest of the "Scrubs".'

Over the next half-hour, Ben Hallett showed me the farrowing room, the fattening pens with electronically controlled feeders, the automatic slurry scraper, the heating system, water sterilizer, ventilation and air extraction equipment, and finally the main office, complete with a vet's desk for the writing and filing of health reports.

'I hope you won't have much to do here, Mr Lasgarn,' he said when the tour was complete. 'Health care will be the main priority, and if it all works well there should be the minimum of bugs. As for welfare – I want you here at least once a week to make your own personal check. If you see anything, and I do mean anything, from wounds, sores, loss of condition in the pigs, to poor hygiene or bad feeding practice, tell me and I will make damn sure it is put right. Loss of natural freedom is the big sadness of the system, I will agree, but I aim to make conditions as near perfect as possible in every other respect.'

'What about early weaning at five days?' I queried.

'They do it with calves and no one complains,' he replied.

Then he made some tea and we talked over generalities for some time.

Despite my misgivings, I felt Ben Hallett was honest about the enterprise, and humane as well. I was sure we could get on together.

'When do they come in?' I asked.

'Week on Monday,' said Ben. 'Come down in the afternoon and you can give them all the once-over. That is . . .' he added, picking up the mugs, '. . . if you don't mind doing the work.'

'I'll be here,' I said.

'Good.' He held out his hand again. 'I'm glad. I know you don't agree with it – most vets don't – but if it has got to be done, it is up to the likes of you and me to do it as best as we can – eh! See you week on Monday.'

As I drove back to Welbury I pondered the question in my mind. Would I like to work there or would I not? I really did not know.

And neither did I find out, for three nights later the whole enterprise was burnt to the ground.

12

I learned of the disaster from Tom Collet, the bailiff at Granstone, when I called the following morning to vaccinate some calves.

'Burnt like a matchbox,' said Tom. 'You could see the flames from here.'

'I was only there on Tuesday,' I said, 'talking to the new manager.'

'Double tragedy,' he sighed. 'Poor devil.'

'Double?' I queried.

'Collapsed with a heart attack when he saw it. Fighting for his life now he is, in the County Hospital.'

I could hardly believe it. Ben Hallett, so enthusiastic about the project when I had last seen him only a few days before.

'What caused it, Tom?'

Tom Collet shrugged his broad shoulders.

'*Who* caused it – that's more like it. Farm fires are electrical faults mostly – we had one here a few years back. But a new place like that, wiring should be perfect.'

'There has been a lot of antagonism,' I agreed. 'But people surely wouldn't go to those lengths around here, would they?'

'There's all sorts of odd-balls about these days,' said Tom, 'but there's summat fishy, because the police have already been around here asking after the Belmont woman.'

'Who's that?'

'Bit of a cranky bird that used to rent Mill Cottage – but she's scarpered. One of these dippy animal lovers, wouldn't eat meat or eggs or even wear anything that had to do with them . . . what d'ye call that sort . . .'

'Vegan,' I said, thoughtfully. 'Her name wouldn't have been Lydia, by any chance?'

Tom rubbed his swarthy, stubbled chin. 'I think it was, now you mention it. Did you know 'er?'

'Not really,' I said; then I was just about to tell him of her outburst at the Women's Institute meeting, but thought better of it. Hearsay can often lead to false incrimination – but as I worked on the calves, I could not help but feel rather uneasy about the little Vegan lady.

It took about an hour to complete the injections and I finished just on eleven o'clock.

'Have a look at Grace before you leave,' said Tom. 'I brought her up last night from the Parks. She was standing about by herself all day and since she's come in she hasn't eaten a mouthful. Must be coming on ten year old now and never so much as 'ad a breath of trouble before; but she's not a right 'un by any means. Old gel's got that worried look on her face.'

His last descriptive symptom may have sounded comical, but for those who know about cows it is a definite sign, even though not one found in veterinary text books.

I collected my medical case from the car and we went through the wide stone archway to the loose boxes.

Granstone still had buildings of great character, befitting such a long-established country estate. The masonry was hewn with dedication, even though it was just to house cattle. All the woodwork was made from Granstone trees, matured and stripped in the mill, then fashioned by a generation of estate carpenters into solid doors, beams and window frames. The hinges and latches themselves were works of art, designed and wrought in the smithy, and each one sound and perfectly fitted.

I always enjoyed working in such surroundings, for the atmosphere of tradition seemed to rub off on me; one felt more deeply a part of the rural scene, whereas in modern units the commercial aspects overrode everything else.

Grace, too, epitomized this wealth of character, for she was one of the old-fashioned types of Hereford, reminiscent of the oil paintings on the walls of Lord Pendleford's study. Of course, artists of that period exaggerated the physical qualities, for quite often their work was commissioned in the nature of sale publicity, before photography took over.

For this reason, they shortened the legs and narrowed the head in such a manner that the length of the body was accentuated considerably.

Grace, though, needed little exaggeration, for she was a grand animal: well framed, deep bellied, wide of horn and with a coat of the deepest, richest mahogany.

She was standing amid an abundance of straw bedding, behind her a rack of sweet meadow hay, untouched. Her legs were spread stiffly and neck extended; occasionally the muscles of her hindquarters twitched momentarily and, as Tom had described, she had that worried look on her face.

'Hasn't drunk a drop, neither.' He picked up a large pail full to the brim with water and moved it into a corner. 'Ain't lock-jaw, is it?'

'Lock-jaw' or Tetanus was not uncommon in the county, though horses were in the main more susceptible than cattle.

'She's stiff but not in spasm,' I said. 'Is she in calf?'

Tom nodded, 'About three months, at a guess. She usually takes first time and the bull was put to 'em just before then.'

'Rules out staggers,' I said, that being another condition common in the Borders, manifesting itself in stiffness and muscle spasm due to a deficiency of soil magnesium; but it was confined to non-pregnant females and Grace was not in that category.

On closer examination, which she allowed without any restraint, something that in itself indicated the distress, I found her to be full in the flanks and her coat damp with a light sweat. Taking my stethoscope I listened for some time, but there was no detectable movement in any part of her bowel.

Then I pinched her back.

Normally a cow reacts to this pressure over the spine by

184

sinking on the knees; but Grace resisted and remained upright, letting out a distinct grunt of pain.

I stood back for a moment and re-assessed the situation.

'What d'ye reckon?' asked Tom.

'I think she's got a wire,' I said.

Tom Collet gave a low whistle. 'We gave up baling with that stuff years ago, but there is a lot of rubbish down on the Parks these days, especially where the ground runs down to that lay-by near Welbury turn; you'd never credit the tack that gets slung over the hedge. Well, Mr Lasgarn, what's the next move?'

'Up on slats,' I said. 'That is the first thing – but if it doesn't work, she is going to need an operation.'

A 'wire' is a general term for any sharp foreign body that, by misfortune, a cow may chance to eat. When straw and hay was made in the early days, fine wire was used to bind the bales together; often pieces would snap off and lie in the pasture or be carried in the fodder and duly consumed.

One might be forgiven for thinking that such objects would be rejected immediately, but such is the grand sweeping action of the bovine tongue and such is the toughness of the lining of the mouth, that cattle often seem insensitive to pricks or pain and the 'wire' is swallowed along with everything else.

Fortunately there is a type of 'fail-safe' mechanism built into the complicated convolutions of the bovine digestive system, in the form of the reticulum. This is one of the smaller of the cow's four stomachs and derives its name from the reticulations or honeycomb-like structure of its lining.

The grass normally goes directly into the largest of the stomachs, the rumen, where it is stored and gently kneaded until grazing is complete, when the cow retires to 'chew the cud'. The cud is re-swallowed, but instead of going to the rumen, now starts on a different route.

On this circuit it passes via the reticulum to the omasum.

The omasum is in itself a most odd organ, looking from the outside rather like a football; however, internally it is comprised of layers of leaf-like projections – hence its nick-name, 'the bible'. Here the cud is pressed into strips between the leaves and in this form presents the maximum of surface area for enzyme digestion in the final 'true' stomach, the abomasum.

We think we can design things, but the Great Architect, when He put the cow together, really excelled Himself.

He even anticipated the odd nail, stone, safety-pin or piece of baling wire coming down and devised the reticulum as a sort of sump, where all solid particles of such a nature are collected, remaining in this antechamber where they are generally unable to foul up the rest of the machine.

The safeguard in the majority of cases works admirably, unless by misfortune the object penetrates the reticulum wall. If this happens, say with a sharp piece of wire, the contractions of the stomachs can cause it to work deep into the body, not only giving rise to excruciating pain, but in extreme cases pushing it forward into the thoracic cavity to pierce the heart sac, with fatal consequences.

The pain of the sharp 'wire' digging into the soft tissue is exaggerated when the cow's back is pinched as I had done with Grace, and the grunt emitted at the same time only adds to the confirmation. As the condition progresses, bowel movements cease, appetite drops and the body attitude of stiffness becomes more obvious as the unfortunate sufferer is reluctant to move.

The first line of treatment may not seem very clinical, although it portrays the commonsense approach of those ministering to sick livestock in days gone by: that is the procedure of putting the cattle up on slats.

The principle is to raise the cow's fore-quarters above the hind by building a small platform in front of her, about eighteen inches high; the common materials used to be cider slats – flat, interwoven wooden boards which, placed across the top of two logs, served the purpose admirably.

With the cow tied short in such a manner so that she cannot pull back, she stands, front end up, allowing the weight of her great innards to fall backwards inside her abdominal cavity, thus taking the pressure off the reticulum and the intruding piece of metal.

In due course, usually about three weeks, the metal, if it remains static, heals over with scar tissue in such a way that it is rendered immobile and its penetrating effect neutralized.

If the 'slat' method is going to be effective at all, the pain usually recedes in a few days and appetite returns. If it does not, then more severe measures are necessary in the form of a rumenotomy, a surgical intervention to fish out the offending object.

Tom was pretty confident he could rig up the required platform and said he would get it organized straight away.

'I'll come back in forty-eight hours,' I told him. 'We should know by then, which way things are going.'

As I left Granstone, I really did hope that the old-fashioned cure would work; if it did not, the task of surgically removing the cause of the trouble would be formidable, for Grace was easily one of the largest Hereford cows in the county and searching for a 'wire' inside her would be looking for a needle in a very unusual haystack indeed.

That afternoon I went to look at Barrington.

The firemen were still damping down, but as Tom had said, it was like a burnt-out matchbox – an incredible and rather frightening transformation from a technological wonder to a heap of smouldering ashes.

'Pity it was empty,' said one of the firemen as I was picking my way through the destruction, 'there'd have been roast pork for all of us!'

It was a sick sort of joke, but not without its irony, for that, so legend has it, was how 'roast pork' was discovered when a pig-house in China caught fire.

Paxton showed little emotion when I called at Donhill to say how sorry I was; something I felt it was only decent to do. He annoyed me by saying that the place was insured and, anyway, I was probably more sorry that there would be no vetting to do there now. That was his way, and I was not really put out; but he did surprise me with his next comment.

'In my younger days I would have said "sod" them and rebuilt one twice as big,' he said with a wry smile.

'You think it was arson?' I queried.

He nodded. 'You were right, Lasgarn. I don't need it.'

'You did say if you didn't do it, someone else would,' I reminded him.

'Then let them do it,' he said. 'I'm finished.'

Like an old bear, mellowed with age and weary of struggle, Paxton had given in for the first time I could ever remember and turned his back upon a challenge. Although in many ways I was sad to see the old campaigner back off, on this occasion I felt relieved, though a trifle guilty: for the demise of Barrington, even before it had become fully established, had absolved me from testing my own principles – for the time being at least.

* * *

One of the great joys of working in the Borders was the variety in the scenery and character of the countryside. Whilst in the morning I might find myself working in Elgar's England, amongst the rolling, fertile acres within the shadow of the Malvern Hills, in the afternoon I might be driving along the ribbon of road that skirted the bare landscape of the Black Mountain.

And as the terrain became bleaker and less hospitable, so did the living. Most of the upland folk practised their craft with cheerful stoicism – 'Hard earned on the hill, easy spent by the river', so the saying went – though the more affluent farmers of the lowland would counter such accusations of extravagance by pointing to the miserliness of those roosting above them. Whereas Herefordshire Disease was a recognized clinical entity of low body magnesium resulting from excessively lush pasture, thin upland cattle suffered from Radnorshire Disease, which was facetiously known as 'going too long between meals'.

No matter, I enjoyed the company and the work in both

situations. Each possessed its own geography, husbandry, intrinsic quality and character; and when it came to clients, each had its share of the good, the bad and the downright awkward.

If Paxton represented the latter in the better favoured areas, then Aneurin Butt was his counterpart on the mountain, but any visit to the Beddrod, to bandy with Aneurin's truculence, was more than compensated by the drive up the valley. The climb was not far short of 2000 feet, the road winding upwards past the 'Moon and Sixpence', where mountain walkers refreshed themselves, past the ruins of the Abbey where monks of old had toiled and worshipped until the marauding Welsh swept down from the hills and put an abrupt stop to it. As one neared the head, the valley narrowed, the crests of the bordering escarpments leaning over to shut out the daylight – a feature which only served to enhance the glorious panorama when one emerged onto the final ridge before heading down to the plateau.

Thus it was the following day, when I made my way to the Beddrod to attend to Aneurin's mare, Bronwen, a cobby sort of animal and as miserable and unco-operative as the old man himself. She was, however, his sole form of transport, apart from a dilapidated Ferguson tractor, and, due to a lameness and her relative importance to his survival, he was reluctantly forced to seek professional assistance.

When I rounded the highest point of the valley road, I pulled onto a gravel patch where many a motorist was compelled to stop to savour the natural beauty of the surroundings. My eye caught a pair of buzzards gliding in the thermals, fingery wings outstretched, dipping gracefully into the buoyant atmosphere.

Winding down my window, I could just pick up their plaintive 'mewing' call – shrill and mysterious, yet so evocative of the wild countryside in which they lived. Down along the craggy shelves, I gazed at the sheep dotted about in all directions, the ponies, tails a-flicking, browsing on the tight heathery sward; then suddenly I noticed smoke.

It was a grey-white column, ascending without deviation into the sky and as I followed it to its source, the sight that met my eyes was quite incredible; for there on the edge of the plateau was what looked for all the world like an Indian settlement – at least at first glance it appeared so. On further examination the teepees were nothing more than shacks constructed from tarpaulins over poles, not in any way as elegant or, in appearance, as weatherproof as the Indian style.

Around the perimeter, rather like a wagon train drawn up in a circle for protection, was a most odd collection of vehicles. Buses, single and double-decked; caravans and caravanettes; some just the carcases of vehicles, devoid of wheels and engine, but yet inhabited.

To get to the Beddrod I had to drop down to the plateau and pass through this 'circus' and, with some fascination, I set off towards it. I could see that my approach had already been observed, for several figures had appeared from the tents and vans and stood lining the road. There seemed a preponderance of children, lurcher dogs, bearded men and tall, gaunt women, and as I neared I could see they were not Indians or even gypsies, but hippies – though driving through, I did feel a bit like 'paleface him come' and was quite relieved to get clear of the area without any arrows in my hat.

There was no road to the Beddrod, just a steep, rough path, and leaving the car at the bottom I commenced my ascent. The name means tomb or burial place, probably of Celtic origin, and apart from the personality of the present incumbent, which seemed in keeping with the place, after climbing to the top one often felt in need of a resting place oneself, if not of such a permanent nature.

As if to mock my exertions, running boisterously and happily in the opposite direction was a mountain stream. A joyous little thing, it encapsulated all the freedom of the region in its bubbling pace and song; yet like a child growing up, it would later broaden and deepen in the lower reaches until it merged with the River Wye, to become silent and serious, grand in its motion, powerful in its flow, yet without that spark of happiness it relished when first it tumbled from its source. As I puffed and sweated on my way, it struck me that its course resembled human life – as we grow older, the fun goes out of things.

Absorbed in these melancholy thoughts, I raised my eyes to the whitewashed farmstead and buildings up ahead, and saw Aneurin waiting impatiently for me. Why was it necessary for him to be part of such an idyllic scene? I pondered; but then, as the Good Book says, 'God moves in a mysterious way, His wonders to perform' – and a good thing, too, for on many occasions He had beaten me with His reasoning.

Aneurin was at the peak of his miserable form and argumentative from the beginning. He was anti- everything: Common Market, Conservation, Conservatism, Tourists and Taxmen; but on this occasion he was railing against the hippies. As I pared away at the sole of Bronwen's affected foot to ease the stone bruise beneath, he ranted on about them being nothing but parasites on society, sitting on their arses all day, full of germs and fleas and getting high on 'magic mushrooms'.

'Pity them things aren't poisonous,' he whined. 'Rid us all of them vermin.'

He knew about vermin, for he was a great trapper, snarer and the scourge of any living thing that dared cross his land.

Like the sickening keeper's gibbet I had once come upon in my youthful days in a woodland glade near Monmouth, his sad trophies were all around – squirrel tails nailed to gates, stoats' carcases impaled on railings, rabbits' paws on doors and, in his garden, hanging like black feather dusters, dead crows swinging in the wind from strings on sticks.

How a man could live amid such beauty and yet be so vindictive towards nature and his fellow humans I failed to see, but philosophically I dismissed him as just another piece in the colourful jigsaw of humanity that made up my country practice.

Bronwen, for her part, had made my job as difficult as possible by leaning into me with all her weight, and Aneurin, during the entire treatment, despite my constant requests, made little attempt to get her to 'stand up'. So when I eventually got back to the car I was hot, disgruntled and had an aching back.

I sat for a while to recover, then set off slowly down the road and once again towards the camp.

Maybe it was the fact that Aneurin and his wretched horse had already put my dander up, which made me in turn somewhat belligerent, for when I reached the collection of dilapidated habitats, I was most annoyed to find the road blocked by an old van. Leaning against the cab was a sinister-looking fellow; his head, unlike many of his male associates, was shorn in the manner of a monk, but a thick wiry beard, which enveloped most of his lower face, compensated for the thatch he lacked on top.

He was clad in a rust-coloured jerkin with a tartan scarf knotted at his throat. His trousers were so tight, they must have been sprayed on to his spindly legs, which terminated in a pair of giant climbing boots whose inordinate size threw his whole figure completely out of balance in a quaintly comical fashion. He was dragging upon a very thin cigarette and made no attempt to move as I drew near.

It was obvious that he was in my way, that flashing the lights or blowing the horn would be rather stupid gestures. So I drove right up to him, nearly on to his boots, and sat there waiting. If he could be bloody-minded, so could I; he had picked the wrong day with me and I could feel my steam rising.

'Shaven Head' took a further drag, inhaled, blew a column of smoke menacingly in my direction, looked down at his boots and then back at me.

By this time about twenty of the community had gathered, standing in small groups. Some of the women held tiny babies in their arms, whilst the men moved forward in a noticeably threatening manner; two of them, I could see through my mirror, were standing behind the car.

Whatever was coming next, I was outnumbered. If I revved up and tried to round the road block, I might well jeopardize the safety of the women and children and, to be fair, as yet there was no reason to panic. But the shroud of Aneurin's ill-will and Bronwen's awkwardness still lay upon me, so I sat silently and just glared at them.

After several minutes, 'Shaven Head' finished his cigarette and flicked the remains away, then spat forcefully on the ground. It was an arrogant gesture, but he had done it on the ground and not upon my car, so I felt points were still even.

Then he came round and stood by my driving window and, with a wave of his grimy hand, indicated that I should open it. This I did, but only a few inches, and he lowered his head to the gap.

I do not know what I really expected, but when he did speak it was quite a revelation.

'I understand you are a veterinary surgeon,' he said, in a clear and most precise Oxford accent. 'I wonder if I might avail myself of your professional services?'

For a moment I was quite confused. I had never expected such a polite reaction – all the signs up to then had been hostile; there was a catch, I was sure, but where?

'What is your trouble?' I asked cautiously.

'If you would be good enough to accompany me, I will show you,' he offered.

Though I did not feel I had reacted in any obvious manner, he must have sensed something.

'We won't bite you,' he said, with a smile.

His remark left me feeling rather foolish, so I got out of the car and followed him through the gathering into the depth of the camp.

They all watched me intently, the women with softly dreamy expressions, the men wary and on edge. One of the smaller children, in running to follow us, tripped and started to cry. I turned to look and as I did so, my eye caught the face of a girl standing a little way off, near a faded yellow caravan. It was a pale, sad face, partly obscured by a shawl, and she turned away as soon as she saw I had noticed her; but it was a familiar face and I knew it – it was Lydia, Lydia Belmont from Granstone. I was sure of it.

'This way,' 'Shaven Head' was calling from the doorway of an old bus, painted in rainbow colours, all the windows, save the driver's windscreen, blanked out with whitewash.

I followed him into the squalid interior – it looked like an indoor rubbish dump and smelled about the same; but he stood with his back to the body of the bus, blocking the view, and motioned to the floor.

There in front of me was a large cardboard box and, lying in it, brown eyes shining, ears erect, its chest heaving with nervous anticipation, lay a young fox with a bandage around its hind leg.

'You do deal with wild animals?' he asked. I nodded. Then he knelt down and gently stroked the little creature. 'He was caught in a snare,' he continued. 'Barbaric devices, but he knew we were his friends, for though he was naturally terrified he has never shown the slightest aggression towards us.'

'How long have you had him?' I asked.

'The night before last,' he explained. 'Under the hill.' He nodded his head towards the Beddrod. 'Why can't people live and let live?' Then he started to unwrap the strips of sheet that had made up the bandage.

I suppose I could have tried to argue rationally that foxes attack sheep and for this reason they have to be controlled; but the fact that it had been snared incensed me too, for that was how I had lost my first cat, Boggy, and I've hated them and those that lay them ever since.

'It's a bad wound,' he said, as he unwrapped the last remnants of the covering. 'I have packed it with comfrey, but it is getting beyond my capabilities.'

Together we lifted the little fox onto the floor where I had more room to carry out an examination.

The snare had bitten into the flesh below the hock and

the skin torn downward, obviously when the frantic creature had attempted to pull itself free. But it was clean and a couple of stitches even at that stage could draw it back easily; fortunately, as there appeared little damage to the deeper structures, there was no reason why it should not heal.

Sadly that was not all.

The lower part of the limb was twisted in a distinctly abnormal fashion and, as I gently manipulated the toes, I detected a tibial fracture – as well as the skin wounds the little fox had a broken leg.

'It will need suturing and a plaster cast,' I told him, following my interpretation of the degree of injury.

'That will involve considerable work,' said 'Shaven Head'. I nodded in agreement. 'And expense, too,' he added.

I stood up, but he remained on his knees, cradling the little fox in his arms; its condition was no doubt a result of Aneurin Butt's callous handiwork.

As I took in the eccentricity of the surroundings, the face of Lydia infiltrated my mind as it had looked when she railed at me in the schoolroom at Granstone.

'The Speaker says – and I quote: "It is my belief that all creatures have a right to survive in God's world, in a way as conducive to their well-being, both mental and physical, as possible."'

Yes, I had said that, though at the time in a rather subconscious manner and, to be truthful, only when she had read my words back to me had I realized what my beliefs actually were.

How often does that happen? Showing one's true colours without knowing it.

All creatures: foxes, pigs, buzzards; sods like Aneurin; pompous bastards like Paxton; asthmatic boys like Billy Bent; frightened 'on the run' Vegans like Lydia; hippies in general and old soldiers like Ben Hallett . . . Ben Hallett. I wondered how he was.

The right to survive.

195

'There will be no charge,' I said to 'Shaven Head'. 'I hate snares, too.'

With his assistance, I mended the limb. Fortunately the suture line was above the lip of the plaster, so that I had no need to leave a 'window' in the cast, which would have not only made the application tricky but reduced its effective strength.

When I had finished, a girl in a blue dress brought me some tea in a large earthenware mug. It was herbal with goat's milk, and though I was normally of the opinion that even China tea resembled gypsy's shaving water, I found the flavour quite pleasant.

'The stitches will need to be removed in ten days,' I explained. 'I have left the ends long so that you can snip them out yourself. The plaster cast is another matter. The limb is very fragile and I think I should remove that; but you will have to bring it down to my surgery in Welbury in about five weeks' time.'

'We may be leaving before then,' he replied, 'but I will ensure that it comes to you for completion of the treatment.'

Then he held out his hand. He did not say anything, but his grip spoke for him – far more than any words of gratitude.

And with that I was pleased. 'There is just one thing,' I added. 'Have you got with you a girl called Lydia?'

'Shaven Head's' jaws tightened momentarily and his features sharpened with slight anxiety – then his smile returned.

'I truly would not know,' he said. 'We all adopt nature's names here. I am Larch and we have many girls – Fern, Breeze, Bluebell and more – yet we never know each other's given names, neither do we know each other's history or background – nor do we care. We accept each other for what we are now, today, not for what we have been or will be.'

'I just thought I saw someone I knew,' I said, 'near the yellow caravan. Do you mind if I take a look?'

'By all means,' he said willingly.

But although there was a girl in the caravan, she was dark haired and tall. And Lydia was nowhere to be seen.

That night, before going to sleep, I told Diana all about it and my concern about Lydia's involvement with the fire at Barrington.

'I think she's in hiding,' I said. 'I'm sure it was her.'

'There is no evidence, Hugh,' Diana rebuked. 'And you of all people should know what suspicion can do.'

'I am sure it was her at that camp,' I said, 'not sure she did it.'

'Either way,' said Di, 'I feel sorry for the poor girl. Now let's get some sleep.'

A sensible idea which unfortunately did not materialize, for within half an hour I was on my way to a mare foaling, and Lydia and her problems were far from uppermost in my mind.

* * *

Morning surgery was pleasant and, apart from being pecked by a budgie whose beak I was trimming, all went smoothly.

Di brought in the coffee. 'Tom Collet has rung from Granstone. Grace is worse and he would like you to call as soon as possible.'

'Did he give any details?' I asked.

'Said she was grunting with every breath and he doesn't think the slats have done any good.'

'That's going to be a job and a half,' I said as I switched on the sterilizer. 'If I'm not back by tea, you'd better come looking.'

Di looked puzzled. 'Why, Hugh?'

'Because I could well be lost inside a Hereford cow,' I said. 'And it'll be dark in there!'

One thing about Granstone, there was always plenty of help. I had one man at Grace's head and one either side of the rump to keep her steady, for I intended to perform the rumenotomy with her in the standing position.

Tom Collet was to be my personal assistant and hand me the instruments as needed.

Grace's left flank was clipped, leaving a hairless area of about twelve inches square behind the last rib. The left side it had to be, because that was where the bulk of the rumen lay; I then froze the muscles with Ravocaine injections.

'Seen this done before?' I asked.

Tom said 'yes' and Will Frank at the head nodded as well; but the two at the rump said 'no'.

'Right,' I said, 'I will explain.'

I always felt this a wise precaution, whenever I performed an operation in public; then if anyone felt queasy, they could opt out at the beginning and not depart at a vital stage in the proceedings with possibly disastrous consequences.

'I shall make a vertical incision about eight inches long, through skin and muscle and into Grace's abdomen,' I said, demonstrating the site with the handle of my scalpel.

'Then I shall incise the rumen which lies underneath and retain the edges of the cut with this metal frame.' The idea of the stainless steel bracket was to pin the stomach wall to the outer muscle layers, thereby avoiding any contents slipping into the peritoneum. 'When that is done,' I continued, 'I pass my arm through the opening, slide it forward inside the rumen and along to the reticulum – where, if our luck is in (and I have made the right diagnosis),' the latter was a thought and not a comment, 'I should be able to detect and remove the "wire". Okay?'

They all nodded, prepared and understanding, but a trifle apprehensive. As, too, was I, for on occasions such as this it would be impossible to think of animals as 'units'; this kind of interference, even though it is surgical and for the good of the patient, always invokes a quite unique emotion – difficult to put into words, but it is there all right.

A glance about and a quick check to see all was ready and at hand, then I turned back to the operation site.

'Deep breath, Grace!' I said. And, sweeping the scalpel downwards, I split the skin with the first cut.

She was a brick. Hardly flinched at all and I was pleased the anaesthetic had taken well.

In quick time, I was through to the rumen and fixing the frame. After the removal of a few handfuls of partly digested grass from the opening, I took off my apron.

To get the fingers as far as the reticulum one needs to be at full stretch, and the slightest impediment of clothing around the shoulders can hamper one's passage.

Lubricating my bare arm, I gently inserted it into the depths of Grace's gut.

It was an odd experience, to say the least; but like many internal procedures in animals, the objective takes precedence over any distasteful aspects.

Soon I felt the floor of the reticulum, recognizable by its honeycomb pattern. Grace did grunt at this point, and who would not with a vet's arm tickling your liver? Yet her reaction made me confident that I was near the source of the trouble.

I searched about the floor with the tips of my fingers, but there was nothing abnormal, save a few small stones that could cause no trouble. I had fully expected to feel the spiky end of a piece of wire, or even the flat head of a nail – but there was nothing.

'Any luck?' asked Tom.

'No,' I said. 'Just some stones.'

Perplexed, I was about to withdraw my hand when I decided that the least I could do was gather up the stones anyway, so I started to scoop them loosely in my hand.

They all came except one. I flicked it several times with my finger, but it would not budge – and each time I did, Grace grunted loudly.

'You'm touching something a bit tender,' said Will, at the head. ''Er don' like that.'

Mystified now, I released the other stones to concentrate upon the single resistant one. Getting my nails beneath it,

I attempted to prize it from the reticulum floor, and it came, but with it a long, fine shaft.

Cautiously, with the object enclosed in the palm of my hand, I brought it into the daylight.

'What is it?' asked Tom, peering over my shoulder.

'It's a hat pin,' I said and, stooping, washed it off in the bucket of disinfectant. 'It is, you know. Look, there's a little glass knob on the top – no wonder she grunted.'

'Some old lady sparkin' in the Parks,' said Will. 'Dropped 'er 'at as well as 'er knickers.'

The lads laughed, country fashion.

'Give us look,' said Tom. He took the pin and held it up to the light, then he blew on it to clear the liquid. 'This ain't no hat pin,' he said, finally. 'This 'ere is the old man's stock pin, what he lost in that fall!'

'Never!' I said.

'Pound to a penny,' said Tom.

The others craned to see. 'That's 'im,' said Will. 'I seen His Lordship with it many a time.'

'You'd better give it to him,' said Tom, handing it back to me.

'Yes,' I said, 'I'd like to . . .' pondering the consequences of my find. 'It will be a relief for someone I know.'

'Relief for this old cow, already,' said Will. 'Look at her face.'

Then suddenly I realized that Grace was my main concern, and set to and closed all the gaps.

Lord Pendleford was in the vinery, talking to his grapes; Conniston, his butler, showed me through.

His Lordship was a well-built man, red of face, with a shock of white hair, moustache and abundant eyebrows to match. Always heavily tweeded winter or summer, he was a great sportsman, bon viveur and in conjunction with the latter, an authority on fine wines. At Granstone he had extensive vines under glass, which he had developed over the years, and he produced his own vintage which, as English wines went, was highly thought of.

'Ah, Lasgarn!' He beckoned. 'Come and look at this.'

He was holding delicately in the palm of his hand a bunch of rich red grapes, still attached to the vine.

'Beautiful, don't you think? Mourvedre – just reaching their best.' He put his nose close to them and breathed in ecstatically. 'Superb,' he said, closed his eyes and savoured the aroma once more. 'Now then!' He re-opened his eyes very widely, making his eyebrows rise like the wings of the Tower Bridge. 'What disasters have you to report this time?'

I had to smile, for it was true that whenever I had found it necessary to see him in the past, it had invariably been to explain unfavourable happenings on the estate: such as the time the cattle broke into Victoria Wood and three succumbed to yew poisoning; or the outbreak of pasturellosis in the flock, an acute pneumonia which took many lambs before I could bring it under control.

'I think I can say that this time, the news should be much more acceptable, My Lord,' I told him. Then, holding up my find, I said, 'I believe that this belongs to you.'

He took it from between my fingers, held it at arm's length and squinted; then he looked back at me a trifle suspiciously, before bringing it closer to his face. He rubbed the diamond with his fingers, as if to test its substance and that it was not a figment of his imagination. Then he said:

'Strap me! It's me pin!' He shook his head several times, as if still in disbelief. 'Where d'ye find it?'

'Inside a cow, My Lord.'

He nodded as if that was quite understandable; then he squinted at me again and boomed:

'In a cow, d'ye say?'

'Yes, My Lord. Grace.'

'Grace?'

'She swallowed it.'

'Swaller'd it d'ye say?'

'Yes, My Lord.'

Lord Pendleford sat down upon the retaining wall that fronted the vines. 'I'm getting a bit old for this sort of thing, Lasgarn,' he said. 'Tell me more.'

So I told him the whole story: giving an explanation of how such an incident was possible and the steps I had taken; the operational procedure and the results.

He listened intently, twirling the pin from time to time between his fingers.

'How's the old girl now?' he asked.

'Very relieved,' I said. 'And she should make a good recovery.'

He got to his feet and put his hand on my shoulder.

'A rum tale and no mistake, Lasgarn,' he roared. 'Deserves recognition, that does!' Then he upturned a nearby flower pot, beneath which stood a bottle of brandy and some glasses; pouring a generous measure he handed me a glass.

'Found me pin and saved me cow!' he said. 'A good morning's work, Lasgarn. Your health!'

There was no doubt the old boy was absolutely delighted. He escorted me back to my car.

'Recovering that little gem means a lot to me,' he said, shaking my hand.

'It will mean quite a lot to someone else, too,' I added.

I was thinking of Will Peel and, just in case he might have forgotten, I reminded him of Will's departure as a result of the incident.

'Never wanted the boy to go,' he said.

'The weight of suspicion was too heavy,' I hinted.

'Yes,' he said thoughtfully. 'I know all about that.'

'It would be nice if he could be told that it has come to light,' I suggested.

'Do it meself,' said Lord Pendleford.

True to his word, he telephoned the farm almost immediately after I left and asked Will to go and see him. This I knew, because a delighted young man came over to Welbury that evening.

'Asked me to go back as Head Groom, he did,' Will explained excitedly. 'Crabb's leaving at Christmas and I take over then. Oh, Mr Lasgarn, how can I ever thank you?'

'Thank Grace, not me,' I said. 'She was the one who really found it.'

Over some coffee with Diana, he told us what plans he had for the stables and how he was looking forward to starting back again.

'Thank God it's over,' he said, as he was about to leave. 'Though I do remember what you said that time, about the experience making me more understanding, and I think that could be true; but I wouldn't want to go through it again.'

'Will you still live at home?' asked Di.

'Well, there is Crabb's house, when he leaves. But that won't be empty until Spring, so His Lordship said I could have Mill Cottage in the meantime.

'Where Lydia Belmont lived,' I said.

'Yes. Did you know her?' asked Will.

'Mixed up young lady who is probably going through exactly the same as you did, at this very moment,' said Diana. 'I know everybody suspects her of being involved at Barrington – even Hugh does.'

'That is not strictly true,' I countered.

'I used to meet her when I was out exercising the horses,' said Will. 'We used to talk a bit, but she was very shy.'

'She wasn't shy at the meeting I spoke at,' I said. 'Far from it.'

'What happened?' said Will, with obvious concern.

I told him about her outburst and how the police thought it was arson at Barrington; that her principles had obviously made her a suspect and how she had disappeared. Then I related my experience with the hippies and my possible sighting of her.

'In retrospect, I was probably mistaken,' I said. 'Her face was half covered, anyway.'

'Poor kid,' he said. 'I know how she feels.'

It was a few weeks later when I saw Will Peel again. He was standing at the surgery door holding a large cardboard box.

'I was asked by a young lady if I would bring this over,' he said, a mischievous grin on his face.

He carried it into the surgery and placed it on the examination table.

'I think you will recognize it.' He opened up the flaps.

And recognize I certainly did, for inside was a little brown fox with a plaster cast on its left hind leg.

'The lady,' I said. 'It wouldn't be . . .?'

He nodded. 'She is outside in the car.'

Diana was away at the time and I had to give her every detail of the event that night.

'Will's cousin works for S & G Electrics, and when he went over to Will's place, they got to talking about the Barrington affair, and Will's cousin mentioned that the fire was caused by a faulty motor in the big ventilator fan that had been running at the time – the one I thought was the only friendly aspect of the whole outfit.

'It had been kept very quiet because of the impending insurance case, but arson had officially been discounted.

'Will had been down to look over Mill Cottage that day and had come home feeling rather heartless about moving in, even though it was no real concern of his what had become of Lydia. However, when he heard what his cousin had to say, he remembered his own relief when the pin had been found. So he decided to go up to the hippie camp and see if Lydia was really there.

'When he arrived, they were just packing up to leave, so he took his binoculars and sat on the side of the hill, looking at each person individually, until he spotted her. Then he went straight down and told her.

'Upshot of it was, Will took her and the fox back home to Rowan's Bank with him: she is now in Mill Cottage and I wouldn't be surprised if before long Will was there, too.'

'How wonderful,' said Diana, with tears in her eyes. 'I'm so happy for them.'

I had to agree.

Then the phone rang; but it was something that made me happy, too.

It was a wrong number.

So we turned out the lights and went to bed.

13

One of the delights of vetting in a country village lies in the endless variety of patients that come through the surgery door – and the vet is expected to know about each and every one.

In fact, I am sure that if a travelling circus came through Welbury and the elephant collapsed outside the Olde Tea Shoppe, someone would be sure to say:

'There is a vet down the lane. I'll fetch 'im!'

And of course, I would go and see what I could do, even though elephants did not feature very highly in the Glasgow University curriculum for veterinary science.

Not that I don't get some unusual creatures to treat in my village practice. Once I had to amputate the end of a pet monkey's tail after it had been practically severed due to being shut in a car door. Then there was the iguana that had been splashed with bleach, and the snapping turtle that had lost its snap.

But my most exotic experience was without doubt when an Italian gentleman produced a boa constrictor with running eyes, comfortingly advising: 'Hesa notta poisonous – but donta let 'eem get around your necka!'

There are of course risks in handling any animal, and often the most dangerous are the most unlikely; but caution and common sense can help to reduce injury to a minimum. There are simple tricks, such as giving a budgerigar a pencil to peck whilst conducting an examination: this avoids lacerated fingers and having to smile grimly and mutter with restraint, 'Don't do that, you little bug . . . dgie!'

Many people believe that animals can tell when one is endeavouring to help them, though, over the years, I have had reservations about that theory, remembering the reactions of some of my patients in distress. There have been occasions, however, when I have thought it possible, as with Wilf, the only dog on my books with a criminal record.

I first met Wilf at an identification parade – well, not exactly. It was when Roger Boyne brought the great, gangling, rough-coated Wolfhound into surgery one night and asked if I knew to whom he belonged.

'I thought he might be on your books,' he said.

Certainly I would have known if he had been, for he was a most unforgettable character.

Apparently Roger, who worked in Ledingford, was coming back to Welbury after a late shift. As he drove over the Causeway, a wooded range some four miles from the village, he thought he saw a deer standing in the middle of the road; but on getting out to investigate he discovered to his apprehension that it was a giant-sized dog.

Before he had time to become further unnerved, Wilf clambered in through his car door and lay down on the back seat.

'Frightened the life out of me,' said Roger, quite understandably, 'but he wouldn't shift and was too big to argue with, so I took him home.'

Roger rang PC Packham, but he had no reports of any such lost dog and suggested they came round to me. 'If he isn't claimed in a fortnight,' he told Roger, 'we can have him destroyed.'

'I couldn't have that,' said Roger. 'They said I could keep him and I will do – but the trouble is, he will not eat. I have tried him on all sorts of tinned food, but he just turns up his nose at the lot.'

'I reckon that could be a bit too fancy,' I suggested. 'Judging from where you found him and the fact that he is used to lying low in a vehicle, I think he is a poacher's dog. There have been several deer taken from the Park, according to the keepers, and as for his appetite, if I am right, then he is more used to having his meat on the bone and not out of posh tins. Try him on some lights or tripe, it may do the trick.'

In fact it did, and Wilf – the name given to him by Roger – settled down well.

My theory must have had some substance for nobody claimed Wilf, though three Welshmen with similar hounds were apprehended some miles south of the Causeway a few weeks later on the Fasely Estate, and discovered to be in possession of a deer carcase.

Roger and Wilf became great companions and the Wolfhound improved in condition, but unfortunately not in temperament – at least not when he needed any form of medical attention. Injections he endured reasonably well, just growling menacingly beneath his breath; but any further interference, such as examining his ears or trimming toenails, could be a risky business and I felt very much like Daniel in the Lions' Den. Fortunately Roger could handle him well and, despite the size of the hound's frame and his frighteningly large teeth, I had no real fears.

That was, until the night that Nancy, Roger's wife, rang to say that Wilf had been involved in an accident with a car. He was badly cut about and needed immediate attention; unfortunately, Roger was away and she would have to bring Wilf herself.

I anticipated a pretty ferocious session, for I knew full well that he hated a muzzle, and was prepared to sedate him on arrival; but when he hobbled through the door, carrying his damaged leg, he was a changed character – no snapping or snarling or straining at the leash.

It was a nasty gash, but as I cleansed and dressed the wound, he lay on my table like a lamb. It may well have been concussion or shock that was affecting him, but when I had finished my bandaging, he raised his head and licked my hand.

So there is some evidence that animals know – at least, I'm pretty sure that Wilf did, that night in my surgery.

★ ★ ★

Constantly working with animals, one cannot be unaware of the bonding between them and ourselves. My philosophy that all creatures on God's Earth have the right to survive was very laudable, but it did depend so much on help from one's neighbour. Befriending them in times of need, as Roger did Wilf, need not be confined to domestic animals. This struck me one morning out at Marsh Farm, where I had been called to a cow in calving difficulty.

It had been a strenuous but successful delivery. After I had untangled the confusion of heads and legs, two beautiful Friesian calves were born.

Ken Lewis, the farmer, was very pleased, for the mother was one of his best milkers and since both calves were female, they would carry on the line.

Soon the old lady was on her feet and vigorously licking her struggling offspring.

'No tonic like live calves,' said Ken, as he gently drew the smaller one nearer its mother – and I shared his sentiment.

As I packed my gear, I was thinking of breakfast for which the early morning exertion had given me a considerable appetite, when I realized that young Andrew, the farm lad, was standing beside me.

'I know you must be in a hurry,' he said hesitantly, 'but could you tell me how to rear these?'

He held out a plastic pot containing strips of rag and some cotton wool. At first I could see nothing else, until he parted the rags with his finger to reveal two baby mice. So tiny, yet so perfect. Their coats were quite sleek and their eyes open.

Disturbed by our attention, they pawed at the rags with their delicate pink feet and burrowed out of sight.

'It was when Mr Lewis sent me to get the cow you have just calved,' said Andrew. 'The dog ran ahead and suddenly threw something up into the air. When I got to it, I found it was a mouse nest. The mother was already dead and these little scraps were lying in the grass.' He moved the rags carefully and the little creatures scurried around the pot. 'Probably seems a bit stupid,' he said, 'seeing as how there are hundreds of them around the buildings eating away at the corn; but I just didn't have the heart to leave them there.'

'It's not stupid at all, Andrew,' I said. 'Every creature deserves a chance. Considering their eyes are open and their coats are established, they must be at least ten days old. Warmth is the main essential and to keep up their energy try some diluted sugared milk in a shallow lid; you could add a little cereal later and something for them to gnaw upon, like a piece of apple.'

'What about cheese?' asked Andrew.

'Oddly enough, although mice like it, I have known it upset pet mice, so I don't think I would give them any. That is about as much as I can suggest.'

He thanked me. 'I'll give them their chance, Mr Lasgarn,' he said.

As I drove home, my thoughts of breakfast took second place to Andrew and his mice. I had got great satisfaction from assisting the birth of the two fine calves, and Ken Lewis would get his from bringing them up to strengthen the herd and in time improve its profitability. But how marvellous that caring for two baby mice in a plastic pot could give equal satisfaction to a young lad.

Sometimes, though, that peculiar satisfaction only comes after much heart searching. Late one afternoon, Mrs Dean and her two sons turned up unexpectedly at surgery.

'Sorry we haven't made an appointment,' she said, 'but Michael and Tom were so concerned and insisted that we come straight here.' She handed me a small cardboard box and I led the three of them into the surgery.

'I feel so humble about this,' she said. 'We were coming back to the village and the boys spotted it from the car as we came over Foley Bank. Tom said it wasn't well, though how he could tell at that distance I do not know. Well,' she continued, 'I told them it would be all right and did not bother to stop; but by the time we had got home, they had kept on so much, I felt quite heartless. Then Tom said: "If I was lost and wasn't well, I hope someone would find me."' Mrs Dean sighed deeply. 'That did it,' she said. 'I felt so desperately guilty that I got a box and went back. It was still there and I picked it up and we brought it to you.'

I peered into the container to find a little scrap of fluff lying in the corner – it was a baby rabbit.

It was slightly concussed and gave no struggle when I examined it; fortunately there were no broken bones; but its nose was reddened and bruised, as if it had suffered a blow.

'Might have been scared by the traffic and run into the kerb stones,' I suggested, remembering that the council workmen had recently installed some up at Foley Bank to prevent the verge subsiding. 'However, a little glucose and water will soon counteract the shock and it should recover.'

'Can it stay at our house, Mum?' pleaded Tom.

'But it is a wild creature,' said their mother. 'It wouldn't like to live as a captive.'

'We live there an' we are not captives,' said Michael, wiping a tear from his eye. 'It would be our friend.'

'What do you think?' appealed Mrs Dean.

It is not the big things in veterinary practice that take the most handling, but small happenings, where emotions and involvement are so sensitive. Here were two youngsters intensely concerned about a small wild creature, and feeling the need to care for and protect it; such sentiments might well influence their whole outlook in the future and if incautiously treated, could affect the compassion they had already shown.

It is sometimes difficult to decide whether the natural but precarious freedom of the wild is preferable to the restrained security of becoming a pet, but there are circumstances when, to my mind, it is not only acceptable but beneficial to both parties; this case, I thought, was one of them. The rabbit would have been most unlikely to survive had the boys not cared about it.

However, before I could answer, Tom, who had taken the tiny creature from the table and was cuddling it to his chest, said: 'If we kept him, we could call him Lucky, couldn't we, Mum?'

210

Mrs Dean smiled and nodded, and I could see that the little rabbit had found a new home. As for his name – Lucky seemed quite apt.

* * *

Most people care for animals, though often in different ways: like Paxton whose affection for all things was masked by brashness and self-importance, or like Lydia with her outspoken, often irrational emotions.

As a vet, I have always contended that a sentimental love of animals is not enough in itself – one must have respect for them. But although throughout my career I have endeavoured to live up to this precept, there was one particular time I found the balance very difficult to maintain.

It started with a tuberculosis breakdown in the Balmoor Dairy herd. Herefordshire, like most of the country, was now designated a 'clean area', Mycobacterium Tuberculosis, the germ that had so long ravaged both human and animal bodies, having been practically eliminated. In the countryside, dairy and beef herds were no longer subject to the insidious wasting disease, thanks to the co-operation of the farming community, the Ministry of Agriculture and country vets, all of whom had taken part in the fight.

It had been a long struggle and far from easy. Cattle were subjected to a test involving the injection of an innocuous extract of the tuberculosis germ, called 'tuberculin', directly into the skin of the neck. Whilst this was incapable of producing any form of tuberculosis, it had the capacity to act as a sensitizing agent in infected cattle, causing a reaction in the form of a swelling at the point of injection.

It was by this method that 'reactors', as they were termed, were diagnosed, eliminated from the herd and duly slaughtered, with some financial compensation given to the farmer.

Although the scheme was highly commendable in the long term, making milk a healthier food and dramatically reducing tuberculosis in the human population, in the short term it posed considerable difficulties in the smaller dairy herds, when half the cattle failed the test. The financial effect was often serious, for the compensation was not really adequate, paying out only on 'cow value' to which there was a not over-generous ceiling price.

This was compounded by the fact that there was no allowance for the shortfall in income through loss of milk, for replacement cows were prohibited until the remaining herd had passed two clear tests at an interval of one month. Sometimes this took ages to achieve, due to the slow development of the disease, with reactors unexpectedly cropping up even though they had passed several previous tests. Yet surprisingly enough, although money matters were of great concern, they often took second place to the emotional effect of having to part with old friends.

In those days there were still the Blods and the Cissies spending their time happily in such places as Lark Pasture or Sleepy Meadow. Sad contrast today, when the only identity is a freezebrand number on the backside, and fields no longer bear picturesque names, but impersonal codes such as A5, K9 and M3.

It was always worse when the cows showed no symptoms of the disease, which could often be the case; but in eradication terms, if the swelling exceeded a certain number of millimetres – a difference of four being often enough – then, no matter how grand a cow looked, how gentle she was, how well she mothered her calf, she went to kill, and that was the end of it.

It was heartbreaking in many cases, especially when a calf had been reared by one of the children and was just coming into the herd. Then, no amount of explanation about it being 'in the best interests of the community' would serve to stay the tears.

Gradually, however, the job was done, the disease suppressed and reactors became a rarity; in some places, such was the success of the exercise, testing was limited to once in every two years. Very occasionally one did come across 'doubtfuls', which were retested but usually passed on the second attempt. Of those that did fail, it was invariably traceable to some contact with one of the few remaining 'unclean' herds in the country.

The Balmoor herd was self-contained, which meant all replacement females were home-reared, having no outside contact with other cattle. So when I turned up three doubtful reactors at the annual test, I had little fear that there was any problem and was confident that, on the second test, all would be well.

But all was not well when I visited one month later to read the results, and to my dismay discovered all three had failed.

It was a Company Farm and the manager Ted Lindley went back through the records. Apart from the Hereford bull that had come from a pedigree herd I knew well, which had never had any incidence of the disease, no other cattle had ever entered the premises.

The Ministry was extremely concerned and, as was their procedure, took over the testing – turning up even more failures.

When the word got round, there was general alarm in the county and constant speculation as to the source of the infection. Everything and everybody, from deer to gypsies, became suspect, but above all was one who has often been described as the oldest landowner in the country: no belted earl or duke, but a creature who never went out of its way knowingly to cause trouble; content within its family circle, tidy in habit and a nuisance to nobody – dear old Brock the badger.

Infection of the species with cattle tuberculosis had recently been demonstrated in the neighbouring county of Gloucester, by the chance finding of a dead badger with advanced lesions of TB. The badger had been found on a farm where intermittent cases of tuberculosis had been disclosed at the annual test, similar in pattern to Balmoor.

Cases had also been detected in other herds in the vicinity, and in a number of them the affected animals were youngsters and had been wintered on pastures in the more outlying parts of the farms, close to badger terrain.

Further investigation following the trapping and slaughter of badgers in the area revealed that twenty per cent of them were carrying the germ. Discovery of lesions in both lungs and kidneys suggested that the infection was 'open' and readily spread on pastures during nocturnal sorties.

There was, however, general agreement that the badger family had first caught the disease from the cattle, but were now unfortunately acting as a reservoir of infection. It seemed rough justice that after becoming innocent victims of the cattle disease, they were to be slaughtered in order to save the very creatures responsible for their involvement.

Naturally there was strong reaction from many quarters in support of protection for these unfortunate animals; especially when it was realized that, according to Ministry statisticians, such a massacre would eliminate at least eighty per cent of healthy badgers.

The proposed action was equally questionable when the habits of badger colonies were taken into consideration, for it was well known that repopulation of vacated setts by neighbouring badgers was a common occurrence, so that, like the sweeping tide, the ground would be occupied *ad continuum*.

There was of course as much emotional hot air as scientific side-stepping, but the observations of some researchers showed that badgers strongly avoided cattle, and in turn the majority of cattle disliked intensely anything contaminated with badger 'products', via which spread was likely to occur.

Yet despite vociferous protests, the practice of trapping and slaughtering badgers was commenced by the Ministry in the infected areas.

The task was in itself exceedingly frustrating, for though old Brock may have appeared an ungainly oddity, he was not without his guile and kept a low profile as soon as he sensed danger, such that many were the man hours expended and few the badgers taken.

In Balmoor's case, it was known there were badgers in the vicinity and moves were being made to investigate them – the methods necessitating post mortem examinations.

Though I could appreciate the logic of the scientific reasoning in veterinary terms, I was not convinced that wholesale massacre of the species in problem areas was the answer. The killing was bound to be indiscriminate and that, to my mind, was unacceptable; on those lines one could argue that the problem could equally be solved by slaughtering the whole of the Balmoor herd. It smacked of double standards: just because a badger was of less intrinsic value than a pedigree cow, the axe fell upon him.

I was against it on those principles – or was it just those? Could it possibly have had anything to do with that night in the Trevethin Wood, many years ago?

I had been involved in a fight at school, with Boxy Potter; I reckon I could have finished him that day, but Miss Pugh caught us at it and took us before Mr Tom Davies, Headmaster.

We both got the 'cut', four on each hand, and when I got home I received another clip from Mother for tearing my shirt.

More annoyed about not triumphing over Boxy than anything else, in the evening I went up into the Trevethin Wood. Hands in pockets, I scuffed along the dram road; this was the remains of the track that used to carry the little wagons full of limestone to the kilns farther down the valley.

The rails had long been lifted but the round bolt-holes could still be seen in the stones where the sleepers had been secured and, head down, full of youthful melancholy, I counted them, one by one.

I sat for a long time on the Sunny Bank, a small projecting plateau that overlooked Abergranog, watching the sun dipping over the Pentwyn tips on its way to Abertillery. From where I was, I had the choice of three ways home: I could go back the way I had come, go on to the bridge at the Ffrwd or cut down through the trees to the Boggy Pipe and cross the river there. I decided upon the latter.

It took me through part of the woodland I had never visited before. Once past the fringe of brambles and gorse I encountered more open ground with hazel and elder trees, defoliated at their base but springing to life above in a thick green canopy.

The sun was now well dipped, the light fading and behind me the moon was already in the sky. As I stood for a few moments to get my bearings, I noticed the sett. At first I took it to be a rabbit warren or fox earth, until I heard the rustling.

Then, out of the nearest tunnel I saw a white head protruding, the nose sniffing for any scent of danger. Without a sound, I scooped down upon my haunches by the butt of a sprawling tree, enthralled by what I saw, for out of the hole in the ground came, one by one, four badger cubs. I knew they were badgers because I had seen them in a book at school.

At first they appeared slightly drunk as they wobbled unsteadily down the bank to a small flat area nearby. They stood in a little circle as if deciding what to do next, then as if suddenly the springs inside them had been released, they went wild. They raced and chased, rolled and jumped in boisterous fashion; round the trees they harried each other, first one way then another, just like a game of 'tag', and all the time 'whickering' away, their tone rising and falling with the excitement.

The area was now enhanced by the shafts of moonlight filtering through the leaves – it was unbelievable in its beauty – and as the badgers continued their merry dance my gloom lifted; I, too, was filled with the joy of their activity, and if anyone felt good to be alive on that moonlit night, it was those four badger cubs and a little boy in Trevethin Wood.

Then, as if to remind me of my own parental discord, their mother emerged.

She, too, sniffed the air, but more persistently than her

216

brood had done; then she scratched the ground and immediately the cubs came tumbling to her side, still bubbling with boundless energy.

Raising her pointed head in the air, she stretched her neck to the limit; she must have known I was about, for suddenly she turned tail and vanished beneath ground with the cubs following suit.

It was dark, the clouds having deepened, when I arrived home and I got into hot water again for being out at that time. I said I had been for a long walk and never mentioned the badger cubs, even to Mother – in fact I never told anyone; it was my secret.

My reaction to the breathtaking spectacle was quite contrary to my nature, for I was a great one to 'tell the tale' and could have scored many points over Boxy Potter, who was my rival at school in more than just fisticuffs. Yet for some uncanny reason I had found my sighting of the cubs so emotive that I could not bring myself to talk about it; it was more fantasy than reality.

I went back many times, but never saw them again, and perhaps that in itself added to the illusion; maybe, too, it was a boyhood memory that contributed in some way to my actions on the night I was returning from Mrs Pebble's at Sollars Green, many years later.

It was just past eleven o'clock when she rang, in high panic, to say that Valentino, her champion and extremely valuable Arab stallion, had collapsed with colic.

I arrived just in the nick of time, for the magnificent animal was about to give his last kick. I stabbed into his vein instantaneously to inject the vital drug, then worked ceaselessly upon his lungs for over half an hour, to restore respiration.

I won the battle and Mrs Pebble was overjoyed.

It was well past midnight as I drove steadily home, my body still quivering from the mental and physical exertion, but my mind elated with success.

I had left the main Ledingford road and started to cut across country towards Welbury, taking the lane that skirted Balmoor. It was narrow and muddy, but I was content to splash along gently, breathing in the crisp night air through the open window.

I had just driven into the dip where the stream runs down from Longmoor Wood and passes through a pipe beneath the road, and as I came up the other side, the lights focused intensely on the greensward. They swept along the base of the hedge as the car levelled, and caught in their twin beams, emerging from the hedge on the Balmoor side, the unmistakable figure of a badger.

I slowed immediately, the wheels sliding on the slippery surface.

Dazzled momentarily by the lights, he halted, statuesque in the glow; then, as I drew alongside, he turned about and lumbered off up the road in front of me.

As I followed slowly behind, I could not help but ponder that I might be witnessing the culprit leaving the scene of the crime, and that before my very eyes might be the cause of the Balmoor breakdown. How dearly the Ministry would like to get their hands upon him, I thought.

The badger had just crossed to the Longmoor Wood side of the road when the lights of an oncoming car appeared. It was going ridiculously fast for the width of the lane and was upon us both in seconds. I pulled mightily upon the wheel and drove on to the verge as the maniac shot by, blasting his horn incessantly; but I had time to notice that he had missed old Brock, who dived for safety into a field gateway, just in time. I cursed the idiot, but was pleased that there had been no accident; though, oddly enough, had he killed the badger there might have been some chance to throw light upon the tuberculosis problem.

It took a couple of manoeuvres to get clear of the sodden verge, but eventually I got all four wheels back on to the tarmac and pulled away.

As I did so, I glanced momentarily at the gateway where I had last seen Brock heading and to my surprise saw he was still there, jammed up against the gate, his wedge-shaped body immobile.

I thought that he must have been hit after all and, fearing the worst for him, backed up, stopped and got out.

But he was still very much alive, for as I approached he started to dig furiously with his claws, generating such force that he sent a shower of mud and stones in my direction; then he went still again.

It seemed odd that he made no attempt to turn or run away, but when I drew closer, aided by lights of the car, I could see the reason.

His head was stuck.

The gate was of metal construction with tubular steel bars welded together by flat metal ties. Near the hinges, the ties crossed at the base, leaving a triangular gap through which Brock had forced his arrow-shaped head, when panicked by the car.

It acted like a yoke and, despite pulling back with all his might, his ears, small though they were, flapped up to impede his extraction.

'That's one way of trapping you chaps the Ministry never thought of,' I told him, pushing the gate slightly to assess how firmly he was caught. My action precipitated another burst of frantic digging, but to no avail.

I could not see very well how much clearance he had, for my shadow fell over him as I bent forward; so I went back to the car for my inspection lamp. As I took it from the boot, my eye fell upon a small polished box lying alongside: the box containing my 310.Baxter humane killer.

Standing there in the peace of a Herefordshire lane that night, a peculiar quandary beset me. To my left lay Balmoor and the herd for whose health and welfare I was responsible. My obligation as a veterinary surgeon was to use every endeavour to diagnose and treat any disease to which they might succumb. And to my right lay a badger who, in the dead state, could well help me to carry out that obligation.

Shooting him would be no problem considering the way he was trapped, and he could be on the pathologist's slab in Worcester first thing the following day.

Yet, what if he did not have TB? If I sacrificed him in

vain, would that prove anything? One badger could not ensure a diagnosis; neither, for that matter, could two; or three; or a thousand if one did not catch the right one.

But he had come off the Balmoor land, which was incriminating enough.

With a great sigh of indecision, I turned my back upon the car and looked up towards Longmoor Wood, safe haven for fox and pheasant, rabbit, deer and . . . badger. The moon was just rising over its ridge, part covered by wispy cloud. I watched its cheery face coming and going through the moving veil.

What of my own philosophy that all creatures have a right to survive? How did that square with Royal College obligations? As a professional, having been 'trained for God knows how many years', as Paxton once told me, I should 'know what to do'. Yet there were some situations that even the wisest of professors could not anticipate – and this was one of them. The possibility of saving a herd of valuable cows against the mistaken killing of a single badger – that was the gamble.

The clouds had now cleared and the moon was bright above; suddenly it was the Trevethin Wood and the white shafted clearing – and those cubs. And as in my mind I once again relived those moments, I wondered how pure professionalism and compassion could ever be compatible – then I turned back to the car.

I did not open the polished box, instead I took my lamp and unscrewed one of the long iron handles from the dehorning shears. With it, I prised apart the metal ties on the gate and set the badger free.

He did not look up at me gratefully, as happens in the films; he just pulled back and crashed through the hedge alongside the gatepost into the adjoining field, and trundled off in the direction of Longmoor Wood.

As I leaned upon the gate in a vain attempt to follow his course, I heard the bells of Welbury Church strike two. I wondered if the Little Owl was still in residence and what he would have thought of it all, but I was too weary to philosophise and set off for home.

* * *

It was a beautiful night, the sky clear and the stars bright as diamonds. Welbury village was deep in slumber and, after parking the car, I walked back down the drive to close the gates.

For several minutes I stood, savouring the tranquillity.

The old church, shadowed by moonlight, had taken upon its weathered stones a softness that seemed to reflect the gentle tone of all about. How fortunate I was to be a vet in this village, that with Diana and the girls I should have come to live in Welbury in particular; our lives had encountered many crossroads, but good fortune had blessed our decisions.

In my blissful state I called out towards the tower:

'Hope you are well, Little Owl.'

But the only reply I got was from PC Packham who emerged from the shadows, on his nightly patrol.

'I don't know about 'im, Mr Lasgarn,' he said in his rich Herefordshire brogue, a slight tone of friendly suspicion just detectable. 'But as for me, and with due respect, sir, I think it was time you was in your bed!'

Epilogue

It is now twenty-five years since we first came to Welbury village. Sara and Joanna are both married and we have three beautiful grandchildren, to whom this last book is dedicated. Jo's little boy, Oliver, is just six months old; Emma is a fortnight younger and is Sara's second. Simon, her first, is four and one of my greatest delights is when he comes to stay.

Together we take a walk, the pattern set by him on our original sortie: it hardly varies a step.

Firstly, down the lane to the long black iron gate at Park Meadow; there we halt; he climbs, I lean and we call to the cattle. They always come at the run, breathing hard and belching great gusts of grassy wind. A mixed and multi-coloured bunch of mostly continental blood, that now-adays sadly is the norm.

Along the bridle path and through the little water-meadow where Wellington lives. Nearly seventeen hands and deep chestnut, the elegant hunter flicks his tail, snorting acknowledgement, before returning to his grazing.

Over the stile and on to the farm – but the dairy herd is no longer there, sold because of milk quota. Instead arable machinery fills the yard: tractors, ploughs and cultivators.

The big black dog is still in residence; much older now, he shuffles out despite his arthritis for Simon to hug, follows us to the church and then, with a friendly bark, goes home.

Simon always asks how high the tower is and, when he is a little older, I will take him to the top.

The view will still be as magnificent as when I first saw it and he, no doubt, will be overwhelmed.

As for me, I shall regard it with a degree of nostalgia, for the panorama of all that is good in agriculture is changing fast.

Changing from green to brown as grazing land gives way to plough. Cattle and sheep to potatoes and corn; country dairies to massive poultry sheds.

I shall not grumble, as many of them do, for change is always about us and transition of life and landscape forever taking place, in Welbury as it did in Abergranog.

I shall just feel content that I was fortunate to have been part of a happy and colourful period in both of those endearing villages.

Fontana Paperbacks: Non-fiction

Fontana is a leading paperback publisher of non-fiction, both popular and academic.

- ☐ Dressing for Breakfast *Stephanie Calman* £3.50
- ☐ The Lavishly Tooled Smith and Jones Instant Coffee Table Book *Mel Smith & Griff Rhys Jones* £3.95
- ☐ Janet Lives with Mel and Griff *Mel Smith & Griff Rhys Jones* £4.50
- ☐ Everything You Always Suspected Was True About Advertising But Were Too Legal, Decent and Honest to Ask *Martyn Forrester* £3.95
- ☐ The Campbell Companion *Patrick Campbell* £3.50
- ☐ Compliments Slips *Diana Copisarow (Ed.)* £2.95
- ☐ Kid's Stuff *Wendy Craig (Ed.)* £3.50
- ☐ Another Bloody Tour *Frances Edmonds* £2.95
- ☐ Nice Guys Sleep Alone *Bruce Feirstein* £3.95
- ☐ All at Sea *Libby Purves (Ed.)* £1.95
- ☐ Fame and Fortune *David Thomas & Ian Irvine* £3.50
- ☐ Sex and Shopping *David Thomas & Ian Irvine* £3.50

You can buy Fontana paperbacks at your local bookshop or newsagent. Or you can order them from Fontana Paperbacks, Cash Sales Department, Box 29, Douglas, Isle of Man. Please send a cheque, postal or money order (not currency) worth the purchase price plus 22p per book for postage (maximum postage required is £3).

NAME (Block letters) _____

ADDRESS _____

_____

_____